D1565565

Think Like a Lawyer

How to Get What You Want by Using Advocacy Skills

Think Like a Lawyer

How to Get What You Want by Using Advocacy Skills

Robert J. Dudley

Nelson-Hall nh Chicago

Library of Congress Cataloging in Publication Data

Dudley, Robert J.
  Think like a lawyer.

  Includes index.
  1. Persuasion (Rhetoric)   I.   Title.
PN4121.D915   158'.2   79–26488
ISBN 0-88229–571–3 (cloth)
ISBN 0-88229–749–x (paper)

Manufactured in the United States of America

10   9   8   7   6   5   4   3   2   1

Contents

1. Introduction   1
2. Frame the Issue   5
3. Distinguish the Undersirable
   and Cite Favorable Precedents   21
4. Argue in the Alternative   29
5. If You Are Going to Play the
   Game, Learn the Rules   39
6. Law versus Equity: Principles
   versus Sympathy   51
7. Simple and Direct   59
8. Discovery   67
9. Don't Open Your Mouth if
   You're Not Getting Hurt   79
10. Do Your Homework   87
11. Anticipate the Other Side   95
12. Get the Facts 103
13. Think Different Ways 113
14. Study Human Nature 123

15. Make a Record 131
16. Put It in Play 143
17. Determine the Burden of Proof 147
18. Demand a Proper Foundation 155
19. Develop a Theory of the Case 163
20. Look for Hidden Motives 169
21. Compromise: The Art of the Possible 177
22. Establish Your Own Style 187
23. Appearances Are Important 193
24. Don't Be Intimidated 201
25. Control and Use Emotions 207
26. Thinking: The Hardest Labor 215
27. Slough It Off 221
Index 225

Chapter 1

Introduction

How do you picture a lawyer? As a practical thinker? A problem solver? A hustler in a three-piece striped suit? An aggressive, self-assured advocate? A careful, conservative equivocator? A counselor? A shyster? The legal profession may yet challenge the snow flake for the breadth of its manifestations. The lawyers' seemingly endless ability to proliferate promises at least a hearty contest.

Lawyers perform many functions. They argue cases. They draw up significant documents like deeds, agreements, pleadings, and threatening letters. They pass upon the safety or propriety of proposed courses of action. They advise individuals, businesses, and governments. They speak to us or for us when we buy a house, break a law, plan for death, seek a government benefit, pay taxes, or divorce a spouse. Many lawyers do not practice law at all but have found other outlets where legal training is useful.

But for all the diversity of experiences, lawyers seem to share a common bond. Several hundred thousand attorneys and tens of thousands of law students share more than a common training, jargon, and perhaps temperament. For want of a better word, let us call it an approach. That approach is the subject of this book.

1

The premise that underlies this book is that we are all advocates much of the time, including many of the situations that are most important to us. It is certain that we could learn valuable skills from the way professional advocates approach a problem and argue their cases.

You, the reader, can contribute to the successful application of the ideas offered in this book by judging which have the most value in the situations that you face. You view these situations firsthand and thus are in the best position to tailor the suggestions to your specific goals. Some, but not all, of the principles should help in any context. Those alert to the possibilities should be able to make extensive use of these ideas because of the frequency with which advocacy situations arise.

You might be seeking a job, a raise, or acceptance of your ideas at work. You may confront a reluctant and skeptical merchant with a consumer complaint. You may want to encourage a friend or family member to pursue a certain course of action. You may be courting someone special. You might become embroiled in a discussion at your favorite watering hole. You may even be wrestling with yourself over the wisdom of some action.

There are enough success books that purport to provide special advice or expertise that have little effect beyond making the reader feel good or accomplished temporarily. This book does not aim to reassure but to supply useful information. No magic formula exists that will transform the passive. Some guidance is possible, but the courage to attempt, the habit of critical reflection, and the lessons of trial and error grow from within the individual. Those who succeed often have not read the success books; those who read the success books often have not learned.

Besides the obvious sources rooted in the law, such as legal reasoning and trial strategy, this material reflects a fusion of the contributions from such kin of legal advocacy as logic, debate, persuasion, salesmanship, and common sense. The treatment stresses the practical rather than the theoretical. The objective is to provide a handbook or a tool and to avoid an academic or philosophical framework. If any philosophy buttresses this approach, it is the catch phrase of the pragmatist: If it works, use it.

Two internal tensions exist within the subject matter that the reader should keep in mind. The first encompasses the irreconcilable difference between conflict and persuasion. Both conflict and persuasion are basic elements of advocacy, but they appear in different forms. The conflict model has adversaries who plead to an arbiter. A trial in court with opposing attorneys arguing to a judge or jury exemplifies this model. The persuasion model involves the attempt of one party to win another over to a different viewpoint. An example of this model occurs when a supplicant appears before a government agency seeking to qualify for a benefit.

The second tension operates between the offensive and defensive positions. Each makes up a part of the whole but demands a separate viewpoint and strategy. One enables and the other prevents. One attacks and the other parries. But they are both sides of the same coin. Their interdependence, however, does not prevent different emphases from producing the best results in a given case.

The tensions between conflict and persuasion and offense and defense sometimes lead to seeming inconsistencies within the material. Different rules apply for different situations. Flattery is an effective tool in persuasion but should not be used to answer an insult. Again, your judgment derived from the facts of the particular situation should determine how the principles in the following chapters can be used best.

Chapter 2

Frame the Issue

*They have no lawyers among them, for they consider them as a
sort of people whose profession it is to disguise matters . . .*
—*Thomas More,* Utopia

Mr. Jones read an advertisement in the newspaper for an apartment which promised in exquisite detail that the tenant would live in carefree comfort and luxury. He became so excited by the flowery description that he rushed over to the landlord. Jones could visualize the wonderful life ahead so vividly that he only wanted to sign the lease and move in.

The landlord's attorney had drafted the lease carefully; an octopus would have envied its all-embracing tentacles. The landlord's interests were protected to the limits of the law.

Jones, the tenant, first saw the apartment when he moved in and was disappointed to discover that it failed to match its buildup. Several months later in the dead of winter, the heat quit and the water pipes froze and burst. Jones decided he had taken enough and he moved out, informing the landlord that the agreement was off and he would no longer pay any rent.

The landlord was unhappy when the tenant moved out, especially because he would no longer receive rent. He knew his banker would not accept this as an excuse when the mortgage payment came due.

After several unsuccessful attempts to untrench the tenant from his position by promises, entreaties, and threats, the landlord sued.

The landlord and the tenant probably believe they are fighting over the same thing. Each considers himself right and the other wrong, and for that reason believes he will prevail in the fight. After all, each only wants his due, what he has coming to him, what is only fair. If we were able to convince others of our opinions and positions as easily as we can convince ourselves, we would surely be in heaven.

You can bet that the lawyers these parties retain will not be fighting over the same thing at the beginning of the litigation. Whether it can be verbalized or not, any lawyer worthy of the name knows that the fight over the battleground precedes the battle and dwarfs it in importance. In the halcyon days of chivalry, the gallant knight would challenge the foe with a confident "Choose your weapon." Due to the guiding hand of a romantic author of fiction, the knight can get away with this kind of bravado, but in the real world it is an invitation to destruction.

So where is the battleground between the landlord and the tenant? The tenant's attorney would like to focus on the promises that the landlord made to entice the tenant to live in the apartment and will claim that the landlord misrepresented the quality of the apartment to induce the tenant to enter an inequitable bargain. He will say that the basis of the bargain was the payment of rent for, at the least, a habitable dwelling. He will stress the unlivable condition of the apartment. He will argue that the tenant dealt in good faith and was victimized by the bad-faith dealings of the landlord. He relies on a contract theory: we had an agreement; you broke the agreement; I do not have to pay you under a broken agreement.

The landlord's attorney finds it extremely difficult to believe that conditions in the apartment could have caused the tenant more than minor discomfort. In sympathizing, the attorney can see that the tenant is confused. The landlord had described the apartment to the tenant as the landlord saw it—with the pride of ownership. The tenant could have looked and judged for himself. But instead, the tenant signed a lease and accepted the obligation to pay rent.

The purpose of the suit is to require the tenant to perform as promised. Any complaints of the tenant about the apartment are independent of the obligation to pay rent. The tenant was not forced to vacate the apartment and did not press demands on the landlord before taking this drastic action. The landlord's attorney relies on a principle of property law that holds that the tenant's duty to pay rent is separate from the landlord's duty to repair.

The tenant's attorney urges the judge to consider the condition of the apartment as the battleground. The landlord's attorney urges the lease as the battleground. The result of the case should follow which of these definitions of the problem the judge accepts.

The battleground is a metaphor for the statement of the issue or issues. According to Webster, an issue is a point, matter, or question to be disputed or decided. Classically, the issue appears in the form "whether or not . . ." Most often, it is not stated this way in everyday speech or argument. But every attempt to persuade or to resolve a conflict contains one or more issues. How the parties settle on what is at issue assumes the greatest importance in establishing how, and in whose favor, the issue will be resolved.

When you are relaxing and just trying to enjoy yourself and have no stake in a discussion, indulge yourself. Let your mind laze. Let yourself drift in the flow of opinions and assertions. Dabble in irrelevancy. Let the discussion take on a life of its own, growing in its own heat as the time passes. When the participants realize they were discussing different issues or shifting from one issue to another, someone can conclude, "Well, it's really just a question of semantics." Everyone will have had a good time and benefited far more than from an evening of television.

But if you have an objective in a discussion, engage in some purposeful thinking at the outset. First determine the precise issue in the conflict. You may find it helpful to express the issue in the classical "whether or not . . ." form to identify it clearly. Your analysis should be as rigorous and thorough as your ability will allow. Precise definition presents as much challenge as any other part of the process. The old axiom about a job well begun is half done applies here.

Once you can satisfy yourself that you know what the issue(s) is, you can begin to work with it. A two-step process follows. Like a dress designer working on a new creation, you must first tailor the issue so that it fits, and you must then model it so that it shows to the best advantage.

Tailoring involves the narrowing of the gap between the issue you have identified initially and the issue that you would like to discuss or dispute. Tailoring alters the core issue you have started with into the issue you can most advantageously handle. You want to convert an objective, neutral statement into a subjective, biased statement. Tailoring represents the difference between what is and what might be. Seizing the initiative here pays off with large dividends. Rather than allowing the issue to evolve on its own or accepting your opponent's version, take the offensive and shape the issue according to what it should be for your own purposes. Try to completely bridge the gap between what is and what might be.

For example, suppose you and your roommate seek relief from the heat. The core issue is whether to buy an air conditioner or a room fan. If you want an air conditioner, you might tailor the issue like this: should we invest a little more money for the extra enjoyment of cool air, or should we make do with a few breezes from a fan? If you prefer a fan, you might state the issue another way: should we satisfy our need for relief with the cool breezes of an energy-efficient fan, or should we splurge on a louder, heavy unit that pumps cold air?

Sometimes, two separate issues will clash and vie for center stage. In this instance, the maneuvering may soften each one without merging them together. Part of the struggle then involves getting your issue debated before the struggle for your desired resolution of that issue begins. Usually, however, negotiations lead to the birth of a new issue from the middle ground of compromise.

For example, you return home tired from a hard day's work. Your spouse lists a number of tasks that are overdue. The issue for him or her is whether to paint the bedroom or finish the income tax. You would like the issue to be whether to go to a movie or take a bicycle ride. If you had gotten your suggestions on the floor first, you would be in a much stronger position. You counter your spouse's list with your suggestions anyway. The ensuing repartee and compromise refine the issue to whether you will watch television and fold laundry or listen to records and pay the bills. You were in a tight spot because your spouse took the initiative with a list of chores, but you made the best of a bad situation by altering the issue to reflect your desire for relaxation.

Modeling dresses the issue with the most attractive accessories in order to present it in the most favorable light. Modeling displays the issue with the characteristics or attributes that strengthen your position. In our domestic example, let us assume that you will advocate watching television while folding the laundry rather than listening to records and paying the bills. You could:

1. Search for all the reasons why your spouse would enjoy the television movie that night.
2. Indicate that you enjoy his or her conversation, and point out that this choice offers a better chance for companionship.
3. Place the unfolded laundry near the T.V.
4. Allow how gracious you are to compromise for your spouse's convenience by giving up a full-length movie out at a theater.
5. Remind your spouse of how much you owe creditors compared to the health of your checking account balance.
6. As a last resort, begin selecting from the dregs of your record collection.

So tailoring gives you a statement of the issue that mirrors your objective, and modeling shows those aspects of the issue that favor your side and reflect unfavorably on the opposite side.

When a lawyer brings a lawsuit, the first stage of the litigation consists of the filing of the pleadings and various procedural matters tied to the pleadings. The complaint, answer, and reply form the basis of the pleadings. The complaint sets out the plaintiff's claim or cause of action. The plaintiff describes a series of facts that caused him or her some injury and a theory of law, such as negligence, the constitutional right to due process, or breach of contract, which redresses the wrong.

In the answer, the defendant responds to the plaintiff's claims. The facts of the complaint can be admitted but explained or an affirmative defense such as self-defense (I punched him but he punched me first), or necessity (I drove my car through your cornfield because that semi behind me lost his brakes and would have used me to stop) can be raised. The defendant can admit the facts of the complaint but contest the application of the law (Your ice cream cone did melt as you passed my house, but so what if there were not more shade trees planted along the sidewalk?). The defendant can counter with other claims.

The reply gives the plaintiff an opportunity to answer the defendant's answer. Any of the approaches mentioned for the answer can be used to respond to the defendant. The replies can flurry back and forth until all subjects of dispute are joined or the parties get sick of the whole business.

The opposing attorneys can resort to many other pretrial pleadings. Chief among them are the motion to dismiss, summary judgment, bill of particulars, and request to admit facts. All of these pleadings operate to narrow the issues that the parties will actually contest at the trial. These maneuvers exist because of the lawyers' desire to frame the issue.

To give you an idea of the importance of framing the issue, consider this. The pleadings frame the issues to be tried. All of the described pleadings function to select which issues will comprise the lawsuit. Roughly nine out of ten cases brought never reach trial but are settled during the pleadings stage. The pleadings stage can extend for months and years before developing into a trial that lasts for only days or weeks.

Without negotiated settlements in civil cases and plea bargaining between prosecutor and accused in criminal cases, our present court system would fall hopelessly behind. Despite our admiration for the consummate skills of the many famous trial attorneys, the overwhelming majority of the action occurs before these artisans step into a courtroom. A solid posture on the issues going into the trial derived from effective pleadings covers a multitude of expert maneuvers and trial stratagems in the courtroom.

Framing the issue is building Yankee Stadium with a short porch in right field for Babe Ruth to aim at. Framing the issue is an actress turning her best side to the camera in every scene. It is conducting business on the golf course or at the tennis club or over a liquid lunch. It is a charitable appeal at Christmas. It is playing on your home field. Framing the issue is taking the high ground and digging in.

When undertaking to shape the issue in your case, think like a lawyer. Think first of jurisdiction, which, in a word, means power. In the law, it is the power of the court to consider the subject matter of the case, the power of the court to bind the parties by its decision, and, indirectly, the power of the court to decide whether or not to hear the case at all. These are called subject matter jurisdiction, personal jurisdiction, and discretionary jurisdiction.

Subject matter jurisdiction concerns the court's power to hear the facts that make up a particular case. For example, a federal court could hear an income tax evasion case but not a murder case. The federal criminal code covers tax evasion, but there is no federal murder statute. When prosecutors are unwilling to try a murder case in the state court under state law, they must resort to another offense to get before a federal court. You then see the unusual result of charging the accused with violating the victim's civil rights by killing him.

Power over the person includes both the court's ability to enforce its determination on the parties and the right of the parties to receive notice of the case and an adequate opportunity to present their side. If both the plaintiff and the defendant live in Boston and the defendant injures the plaintiff in Boston, then the plaintiff cannot file a suit in the court that normally hears personal injury cases in Honolulu because the chances for the defendant to default would increase. Nor will the proper court in Massachusetts hear the case if the plaintiff does not serve a summons for the defendant to appear because the plaintiff might think the chances of winning better if the defendant were to default.

Even if a court has the requisite power over the parties and the subject matter, the court can still refrain from invoking that power in many cases because of its discretionary jurisdiction. Some of the reasons for the court's exercise of its discretion are the following:

1. The plaintiff lacks "standing" and does not have a concrete stake in the outcome of the case. A grandparent does not

have standing to challenge a parent's surrender of a child for adoption.

2. Another court has concurrent jurisdiction; for example, a federal court will abstain from interfering in a case that is pending before the proper state court.

3. The case is not "ripe." It would be premature for a home buyer, on learning that the seller does not own the house, to sue the seller for failure to deliver good title before the date of the closing, as it is possible the seller might be able to acquire good title before the closing.

4. The case is "moot." Events have occurred that have resolved the controversy. An employer reinstates a worker who has brought an action alleging having been fired without cause.

5. The venue is improper, and the case should be heard in another place.

Lawyers seek to fashion arguments based on jurisdiction as the first line of defense in a lawsuit. They try to establish that their opponent has chosen the wrong court or that another court would be more appropriate. If possible the lawyer tries to establish that the opponent is the wrong party to bring the suit or that the wrong defendant has been named. Maybe it can be shown that the action is premature or no longer necessary, or perhaps it can be argued that the location chosen will cause unnecessary inconvenience. Lawyers resort to any preliminary arguments that will prevent their adversaries from arguing the merits of the case or the specific facts.

Likewise, when you confront an advocacy situation, before you become embroiled in the midst of the argument, search for the uses of your first line of defense—jurisdiction. If you succeed in diverting the first clash to a jurisdictional issue, you have added an extra chance for victory. Before you try to convince the authority to decide in your favor, try to avoid having authority asserted at all if you are on the defensive. Or, show that the authority does not extend so far as to cover the subject matter or to reach someone in your position. Frame the issue so that your discussion questions the other party's power to do what he or she intends.

In shifting to the jurisdictional issues, you must realize the need for delicate diplomacy with people in authority. Your general approach should show concern, curiosity, or detached interest in the structure of the encounter and each person's role. Make it seem as if you are discussing the hobby of the one in authority. Do not challenge authority directly or incite this individual in any way. If you dare people to use their authority, they will be inclined to try. If you tell people they cannot do something, they will begin thinking of ways that they can. This holds true even if they want to be fair and maintain neutrality. Many in positions of power do not possess the personal strength and security to resist retaliation regardless of where equity lies.

You can also employ jurisdictional issues as an offensive tactic when persuasion is your goal. You should not raise them at the outset, but once you have framed the issue to your advantage and have progressed into the substantive discussion, well-placed appeals to jurisdiction can lend support to your position. You can call this the "parent-knows-best" approach. In negotiations between parent and child, how often have you heard a parent use phrases such as these? "I've lived a lot longer than you and have had more experience." "I am responsible for you and don't want anything to happen to you." "I only want what is best for you." These are nothing more than jurisdictional appeals that express power over subject matter, power over person, and discretion to exercise power, respectively.

You go to your doctor and say that you are dying. When you are examined, the diagnosis is that you have the flu. The doctor claims to have treated many cases in recent weeks because "it's going around." You believe this because of the doctor's jurisdiction over the subject matter. The doctor has special knowledge because of medical training and from practical experience in treating other cases of the same illness. Any appeal to superior knowledge, expertise, or experience, whether of your own or of some recognized authority, helps tilt the balance in your favor.

If you were to get into an argument with a friend about the fastest-breeding animal, you would perhaps reach into your back pocket for the *Guinness Book of World Records,* which tells you that the streaked tenrec can breed three to four weeks after birth. And then, of course, if you breed streaked tenrecs yourself, you could tack on your own testimonial from experience.

You have found the perfect marketing strategy for new, improved widgets and feel that nothing can compare to its effectiveness— nothing except a different plan favored by your boss, which he describes as he looks at you and raises his eyebrows—which happens only when he is preparing to rain disfavor on anyone who would contradict him. This is exercising personal jurisdiction. This influence over the person could result from economic, moral, personal, or physical authority, among several others.

What can jurisdiction teach us then? It can show us what extrinsic authority, apart from the merits of a case, influences the decision or persuasion. It can uncover the underlying structure of an argument and give us an added basis to avoid it. It can afford additional pressure to support persuasion.

When lawyers speak of a race to the courthouse doors, they mean that more than one court could exercise jurisdiction and that different parties would benefit from different courts hearing the case. The advantages of a favorable setting lead to the race to file in the more sympathetic court. The lawyers would not be running if determining the forum were not a worthwhile advantage.

Some concrete methods of framing the issue by determining the forum have existed for quite a while. A pretty fair philosopher named Socrates originated a technique that enabled him to frame issues for discussion. Plato's *Dialogues* capture the brilliance and effectiveness of the Socratic method, which slowly and unobtrusively leads the other person through a series of questions to the desired conclusion. The questioner controls the course of the conversation at all times and develops the ideas seemingly without effort. Few assertions of fact are made but the information is elicited from the other person. This method lulls that person into accepting the statements that naturally follow from the questions. The other person is more conscious of the statements that are made than of the overall pattern of questions that creates those statements. The person is also more conscious of the statements made than of how this overall pattern of questions accomplishes its end.

This person is much more likely to accept the truth of the statements because he or she articulates them. Advocates respect the Socratic method because the information or answer comes from the other person, and this attribute narrows the infamous credibility gap. But which person actually articulates the statement assumes less importance than the ability of the questioner to control the direction of the discussion and frame the issues. The strength of the Socratic method lies primarily in the control that the questioner exerts in framing the issue.

Teachers have found the Socratic method useful in drawing out students and encouraging class participation. Elsewhere people have overlooked its effectiveness. Normally, we tend to focus on what we have to say rather than on how we can gain acceptance for our points most decisively. We naturally center our interest on ourselves, because we want to impress others with our knowledge and intelligence. Our culture reinforces these basic human tendencies by rewarding aggressors and attention seekers.

Especially in persuasion, but also in a conflict, the Socratic method can accomplish more than reciting the facts and reasons for the other person yourself. Usually, you can persuade more effectively through indirection. The changes in attitude or opinion also will last longer because of the stronger impression made on the other person by his or her own statements.

Reading philosophy causes no known long-term harm to the brain. It would be worth the effort to read the *Dialogues* of Plato to see Socrates at work as he leads his antagonist to the proper conclusion. By studying the development of his arguments, your ability to frame the issues will invariably improve.

A cousin of the Socratic method, which Socrates also used, is the more obvious technique called the "yes-or-no game." In the yes-or-no game you have two options. First, you can shape the question so that only a yes or no response would follow. Second, you can ask a question that requires more elaboration but specifically demands a yes or no response. The latter, a favorite of the cross-examiner, bullies the respondent and can sometimes defeat the objective by alienating the respondent. Usually it is not necessary to be so coarse or transparent.

The human mind naturally shapes the data it receives. Preconceptions, past experiences, prejudices, desires, and a host of other maladies color the perceptions we receive. We selectively listen and selectively understand. We are lazy and prefer to simplify and categorize ideas rather than wrestle with them to a complete and honest understanding. We like plots with heroes and villains clearly defined. We jump at superlatives and compile lists of best restaurants, movies, and writers.

This desire to simplify combines with another phenomenon to complicate the picture even further. This added factor is the inadequacy and imprecision of language. Words can only approximate what they seek to describe. Therefore, language cannot avoid distorting its object. This happens in the best of all worlds. In the world we occupy, people use only a small number of the words available to describe their circumstances, and they often use these words incorrectly. Errors because of faulty usage surpass the distortions inherent in language in the process of selective understanding.

The shortcomings of language coupled with the desire to simplify produce the two-valued orientation which makes people susceptible to the yes-or-no game. People like to label things. You supply the labels—black or white, good or bad, yes or no—and they will probably accept them. People like to classify things. So you supply the categories. A shortcut that bypasses thinking attracts our lazy minds. Ideas are seductive and dynamic in that they act as if they were alive. Like a germ they will grow until checked; without the "antibodies" of competing ideas, they would overrun the mind. An unchallenged idea can live like a king, ruling by dint of its birth and position regardless of its virtue or sense.

The defensive counterpart to the Socratic method and the yes-or-no game is what debaters call "posing the problem inescapably." Before the opponent begins the presentation, you outline the type of case that must be presented in order to satisfy the burden of proof. This approach gives you an opportunity to highlight the negative aspects of the subject before the positive aspects can be presented. You can specify what must be established as a minimum just to remain competitive in the argument, or you can outline the qualities of an ideal case that would be so strong if it could be established that it would make argument superfluous anyway. Using questions, you can emphasize the weak parts of your opponent's position and raise your objections early. Your opponent is forced to argue within your framework or waste time explaining why he or she won't. Your opponent now runs the risk of seeming evasive if he or she shifts away from your ideas, because you have framed the issue at the outset.

A defensive measure called diversion, or distraction, shifts the argument's focus. You can do this in several ways. First, from all of the points that support your opponent's argument, select the weakest one or the one you can contradict most effectively and concentrate on defeating that one point. Once you have disposed of that point with your superior strength, stop. This leaves the general impression that you have bested the entire argument. Second, you can avoid responding to a point on which you are weak and respond instead to a similar proposition that you can refute. Third, raise an unimportant objection. Deny some fact your opponent has mentioned that has no importance for the argument. You can often use humor in doing this and win favor in the personality portion of the contest. Fourth, divert the argument from the issues to personal characteristics. However, this tactic approaches trench fighting where anything goes; it may leave an unpleasant aftertaste.

Another useful tool for the job of framing the issue is slanting. Slanting is the doctoring of a statement or position so that, although it is still literally accurate, it favors one conclusion over another. In its extreme form, slanting becomes question begging. You beg the question when you assume as true in your argument the conclusion that you seek to reach. "I did not steal your money because I am not a thief." You might get away with an argument like that on occasion, but you should rely on more subtle forms of slanting. Selectively incorporate the facts that favor your position. Include facts that support your position even if they are not relevant, and exclude facts that undermine your position even if they are relevant.

Word selection is more important than tinkering with the argument. The novelist Joseph Conrad said, "He who wants to persuade should put his trust not in the right argument, but in the right word. . . ." Words do not remain neutral; they take sides when they go into action. We employ strategy; they resort to treachery. We are patriots exercising our rights to free speech; they are rebels disturbing the peace. We are generous or frugal; they are spendthrifts or stingy. A detergent advertisement authenticates its test by using "U.S. Government soil" to dirty the clothes. Do you wonder if Russian soil would provide a greater challenge? Notice how often buzz words like fact, proof, scientific, and expert appear in this type of ad.

Attempt to associate the conclusion you seek with concepts that already have wide acceptance. Associate your desired conclusion with commonly held values. Likewise, link the undesirable conclusion with concepts and values that provoke disapproval. You may win your argument before the arbiter even turns to the evidence. You will certainly influence the way in which the arbiter looks at the evidence if you have framed the issue with the appropriate positive or negative words.

When is it helpful to be more evenhanded and present some part of the other side? If the arbiter initially leans toward the other side, you may soften him or her and win confidence by pointing out some of the advantages to the other position. When you know the other side will be presented, you can also gain credence by bringing up what you think the other side will mention anyway. You can defuse the explosion by stating these points in a way that most sympathizes with your goal.

Generally, you want to present only your side of the argument if the arbiter leans toward your position, if the other side is not represented, or if you seek an immediate effect and not a lasting one. In this case you should not suggest any competing idea or other interference. Presenting both sides would encourage comparison and choice after reflection rather than immediate acceptance.

In drama, the stage is set before the action begins. The action occurs within the setting and is limited by it. If you do not set the stage by framing the issues, someone else will do it for you, and you will find yourself reacting instead of acting. The saying "Everything is relative" overstates the case but not by much. So much in matters of opinion and fact is relative that framing the issue becomes the single most important factor in determining the outcome.

The law has never favored those who sit on their rights. Advocacy rewards those who press their claims, who initiate, who define the case, and who advance on every opportunity. Frame the issue yourself so that you do not wind up like the hapless rancher in the old western who can only say, "I've been framed."

If God had meant for you to be framed, He would have made you a work of art.

Chapter 3

Distinguish the Undesirable and Cite Favorable Precedents

If you think that you can think of a thing inextricably attached to something else without thinking of the thing which it is attached to, then you have a legal mind.

—Thomas Reed Powell

Your boss summons you to request that you take a business trip to Florida to call on the Fantasy Fruit Company. The boss knows you have been traveling extensively lately and that you have been promised a vacation. The long, hard job you just completed by wrapping up the big Reality Rivets deal is appreciated but Fantasy Fruit requested that you come personally, and the last time when you did not go, the company lost a slice of Fantasy's business. The boss has spoken with the new man, Herb Eager, your immediate subordinate, who is ready and willing to go right away. Especially since you have already arranged a sojourn in the Maine woods, the hot, humid Florida summer does not appeal to you.

You tell the boss that, because the Reality Rivets deal was especially tough, you really need a break in order to perform well on the Fantasy trip. You have been promised a vacation, and you know that the boss does not like to disrupt staffing plans once made. The vacation is really necessary to rejuvenate you and put you in prime form for Fantasy. You also remind the boss that you have gone on the last five trips. Your resistance now is not based on your selfish motives but on your concern about performing at your best. Although Fantasy has requested that you come now, you know their representative will wait until after your vacation and that the delay will improve your bargaining position. The company's previous loss of business when you did not go resulted from the unwise action of your substitute, who has since left the company, and not from your absence in itself.

Besides, you remind the boss that Fantasy represents a small portion of your business compared with Reality and the amount lost would be insignificant. The company should expect more sacrifice and acquiescence from Eager because he is new and has yet to prove his worth. The boss has always enjoyed the Fantasy people and the recreational opportunities in Florida, so if the job has to be done right away, the boss could go and relax and have fun at the same time.

This short fable contains seven statements where a precedent exists or a comparison can be drawn. Four of the statements are favorable to your objective: You've gone on the last five trips; you just finished a long, hard job; the boss promised a vacation; and the boss enjoys Fantasy people and Florida. Three statements are unfavorable: Another worker is ready to go, which reflects badly on you by comparison; the last time you didn't go, the company lost business; and, Fantasy is asking for you specifically. In arguing to preserve your vacation, you associate the favorable statements with your objective and show why the unfavorable statements do not apply or are not significant.

The American legal system follows a common law approach. Common law builds its body of laws from judges' previous decisions in individual cases. When a particular case is to be decided, the judge will note what other judges have done in similar cases. The judge will either apply the established rule of law from the previous cases as a precedent or explain why the established rule does not determine the outcome of the present case. When a judge chooses not to follow a precedent, he or she will distinguish the two cases. A rule of law gains strength as a precedent with each subsequent application, encompassing a broader range of factual patterns.

Since a large number of similarities and differences will appear between any two cases, emphasis plays a major role. The discretion falls to the judge to select from among similarities and differences the ones that will dispose of the case. This creates a vast power. The advocate's job lies in developing the case in a way that accentuates the similarities with favorable precedents and accentuates the differences from unfavorable precedents.

Precedents also guide our actions in our daily lives. Much of our learning operates on the same principles. Despite early morning grogginess, we can squeeze one end of the toothpaste confident that the paste will come out the other end. Experience can be characterized as the body of precedents we accumulate that enables us to choose more successfully among present options. We eat a dish of ice cream, which tastes good. Our reaction will influence later decisions to indulge or not. We get a bad sunburn at the beach and on the next outing we choose to cover up.

The law employs precedents because of the need for predictability. The law does not blindly follow precedents because of the need for flexibility. Predictability and flexibility are two qualities that a legal system must possess in order to respond to the people's needs. Without predictability, people would not be able to conform their conduct to the expectations of the law. The link with past decisions fosters uniform application of the law. Without the flexibility to adapt the law to the unique circumstances of new cases, the resulting arbitrariness would lead to inequity. The judge must preserve the continuity of the law's course and at the same time settle the controversy fairly. How the precedents are juggled to accomplish these goals concerns the advocate.

The advocate strives to compare the present case with similar cases that ended as the advocate wants this case to end. If the judge can be shown that previous judges have already faced the same issues and decided them in favor of the advocate, the judge is given the opportunity to avoid making a hard decision. Making decisions on our own is a lonely, unpleasant task that we have a tendency to duck if an escape route appears. No matter what a judge decides, when competing interests clash someone is going to be unhappy, and the judge has to bear the responsibility.

If a precedent in a similar case is unfavorable, the advocate works on the differences between the cases. He or she fashions as many distinctions as he or she can think of and stresses their significance and importance. Since no case will match up exactly with any other, there is always enough ground to nourish distinctions.

One practical rule predominates when distinguishing the undesirable and citing favorable precedents. When you are weak on the law, argue the facts; when you are weak on the facts, argue the law. (If you are weak on the law and on the facts, look for a way to settle the case amiably and cut your losses.)

A police officer pulls you over for speeding after clocking you at forty-five miles an hour in a thirty-mile-an-hour zone on radar. You cannot attack the traffic laws themselves, as they are clearly proper and necessary. You cannot attack the application of the law to you, as you know that you exceeded the limit. The officer did not estimate your speed; the machine measured it. It is not your word against the officer's. Your formidable foe is a detached, unbiased instrument. You have no case based in the law; therefore you must argue those facts that excuse or explain your violation: (1) The state has sent you a commendation because you have driven ten years without getting a ticket. (2) You need the car for your job and cannot afford the increase in insurance costs. (3) You received a call at work from your wife who has gone into labor. (4) The sign lowering the limit from forty-five to thirty was blackened with spray paint by vandals.

The criminal defense lawyer supplies perhaps the best example of arguing the law when the facts are weak. In the motion to suppress, the lawyer tries to exclude evidence from the trial that could convict the client. Although the facts may establish that the client is guilty, procedural safeguards built into the law to protect individual rights can still provide a refuge.

Here is a hypothetical illustration: although the police know the lawyer's client was shoplifting, they cannot prove it. After taking the client to the station, they begin to question him without explaining his right to remain silent and to consult with a lawyer. He confesses and supplies enough details to convict himself of the crime. The criminal lawyer argues the *Miranda* rule which acts to suppress the incriminating statements.* The client goes free although no one doubts his guilt. The case was won on the law, not on the facts.

An informer tells police that the lawyer's client has a stolen car in the garage. The police get a search warrant for the garage, but they also search the house and find a closet full of marijuana. The drug charge can be beaten because the police exceeded the scope of the search. They could not expect to find a car in a closet, and the warrant limited the search to the garage anyway. The law requires that the warrant state with particularity the place to be searched and the item to be seized. The suspect can afford a weak factual case because the principle of law will protect him. The damaging facts cannot hurt the case because they will be suppressed in any resulting action.

We express the rule: Argue the facts when you are weak on the law; argue the law when you are weak on the facts. Yet we need not narrow its application to legal matters. A fact is a fact, but a law can be more than a statute or an ordinance. A law can be an underlying assumption, an operating principle, an obligation, a theory, an understanding, or any rule that governs the circumstances of a particular situation.

Short of an immutable physical law, you can alter any of these rules with a concentrated emphasis on strong or sympathetic facts. And you cannot always be sure even in the area of the immutable. Such scientists as Copernicus and Einstein have successfully challenged supposedly settled physical laws. Copernicus gathered compelling facts to overcome the accepted belief that the sun revolves around the earth. Your fact gathering does not have to exhibit such sophistication or precision. At the same time, an impassioned "Oh, yeah?" will not rebut a distasteful rule.

---

*Miranda v. Arizona, 384 U.S. 436 (1966), secures the Fifth Amendment privilege against self-incrimination. The United States Supreme Court held that in a custodial interrogation the defendant must be warned that: (1) he has a right to remain silent; (2) anything he says may be used against him; (3) he has a right to have an attorney present; (4) the state will provide an attorney if he cannot afford one. Without these warnings the defendant's statements given during a custodial interrogation are inadmissible in court to prove the defendant's guilt.

You will have more than the basic rule of emphasis on law or facts to help you when you are distinguishing and citing precedents. It is likely that more than one rule will affect the conflict that you face. The more rules involved, the wider your choice in argument is. You can argue for one rule rather than another. You can approach a rule from different perspectives because of the influence of other rules. The more rules involved, the greater the complexity of the case and the better the chance for manipulation, because the resolution is more concealed.

Also, to think of a body of rules leading an independent existence and waiting for the call to resolve a series of facts simplifies too much. The rules themselves change as they are applied. This constant flux enables you to shape the rules more easily according to your view of the facts. A common comment about the U.S. Constitution holds that it is only what a majority of the Supreme Court says it is at any given time. Our rules are not written in stone.

Companion methods to distinguishing and citing precedents include proof by classifying, proof by eliminating, proof by selected instances, transference, and extension.

Proof by classifying operates when you nestle your contention among a class of rules or facts about which your listener already holds firm opinions. You elicit an almost automatic positive response from the listener on such established opinions and aim to spread the residual glow and good cheer on your contention. Salespeople frequently do this by asking a number of questions about their product designed to receive a yes answer. Without mentioning price, they purr on about beauty, comfort, convenience, and so on. When the crunch descends, and customers must put their names on the dotted line and hear the price, the salesperson has softened them into more agreeable frames of mind. Customers later may wonder what they said yes to or why they bought something they did not need. They were probably just trying to cooperate with the salesperson. Proof by classifying is as American as apple pie, baseball, and the flag.

Proof by eliminating lays out all the possible options and shows that they are all unsatisfactory except for the one you are supporting. The advantage to this method lies in your control of the situation. Your list of options may not be all-inclusive and may also contain straw men—options that make your choice look good but that are not themselves solid alternatives. In any case, you are describing the options and can do so from your perspective. Your poetic license is valid.

Proof by selected instances is known in logic as arguing from the particular to the general. You cite a number of examples that support your case and argue that these particular instances demonstrate the validity of your general contention. This approach can be labeled stacking the deck. The welcome problem of proof in citing selected instances involves probabilities. It is impossible to recite all of the particular instances that support the contention. When saying that a certain television show or politician gets the highest rating, the pollster relies on a representative sample of the total viewers or voters. As verification of the statistical sample is too complicated for the bulk of most arguments, you can play statistician and find your own significance in the data.

Transference shifts the prestige or attraction from one thing to another. An actor or an athlete endorses a product. A restaurant or vacation spot is considered "in." A charity converts public approval of giving, or recognition of a need, into contributions for its operation. Recognized authorities, accepted ideas, and admired values influence beyond their own areas of expertise or recognition. Advertisers sell ideas more often than products. They show people enjoying themselves as they use a product. It is this idea of enjoyment that persuades people to buy the product. For example, the glamor of an exotic place disarms the realist and encourages romanticism. But remember that transference can also work negatively to shift disapproval or disrepute.

Extension is a device for carrying your opponent's statement to your conclusion. Extension embellishes the statement according to your objective. By starting with your opponent's statement and constructing the development of its logic, you can neutralize its force or, optimally, contradict the original statement. This device also operates defensively, allowing you to raise distinctions. When your opponent erodes your statement by extending it with a flow of distinctions, you might rather characterize these statements as non sequiturs. By challenging each step of the argument you force your opponent to prove its logical connection with the prior statement. Do not concede analogies but require exact logical connections.

A judge can consider a precedent to be controlling, persuasive, or irrelevant. If you can convince him or her to move the one step from irrelevant to persuasive or from persuasive to controlling, you have done your job as an advocate.

Citing favorable precedents and distinguishing undesirable ones operates on your arguments the way a person's social contacts influence his or her status. When your arguments are seen in the best company, they will be admired and accepted, and when your arguments avoid hanging out with the wrong crowd, their reputation will not be tarnished. Get the right slant on applicable precedents. Enlist the power of association. Make contact with the right precedents. The right contacts can smooth the way for your case.

Chapter 4

Argue in the Alternative

Do I contradict myself?
Very well then I contradict myself.
(I am large, I contain multitudes.)

—*Walt Whitman*

When the principal of your son's school calls you on the phone, he tells you that your son, let us call him Michael Angel, has been suspended for two weeks for carving nude women shouting revolutionary slogans on every bit of school property that he could find made out of wood.

When your son comes home, he insists that he did not do it. He had whipped another boy in a fight, who retaliated by setting Michael up on this false charge. The other boy even stole the knife Michael had bought for Boy Scout activities. Michael contends he could not have been the culprit because he lacked the artistic talent evident in the carvings. Because your son Mike appears sincere, and you believe him, you decide to defend him with the school authorities.

The next day, when you meet with the principal, the guidance counselor, and Michael's teacher, you proclaim Michael's innocence and ask that the misunderstanding be cleared up by reinstating your son in school. You tell them that when you spoke to Mike at length, Mike assured you that he did not carve the shapely subversives. You recount how he was wronged and also remind them that he draws poorly.

The school officials respond that they have several witnesses from the time of creation and that Michael admitted his authorship to the guidance counselor after considerable encouragement. You rejoin that you do not question your son's truthfulness. You wrangle back and forth for an hour, you maintaining your son's innocence to the end. At the end, you walk out with Michael's suspension intact. Perhaps you may feel a bit better, because you stood up for your child and let them know about their mistake. You are a responsible, caring parent.

But you blew it. Too often we look at a case, form a judgment, and argue our conclusion until the frequently bitter end. We become so convinced of the correctness of our conclusion that we think others must draw the same conclusion. We neglect to search for other possible conclusions or other arguments for our conclusion.

Look for opportunities to advance alternative arguments. You will rarely see a lawyer go into court with one argument. Perhaps this accounts for the lawyer's reputation for being long-winded. If so, it is a small price to pay. Because they want to give the judge several chances to see the case their way, lawyers often look for different ways to present their case.

Let us return to the school conference to see if we can construct alternative arguments. Relying on Michael's truthfulness alone would be futile in the face of witnesses and a confession. So you begin with your faith in Michael's truthfulness and you recount his explanation. Then you argue: even if there are adverse witnesses, no one has tested them to substantiate what they say. No investigation has ensued to eliminate the possibility of the witnesses' having ganged up on Mike. How can we be sure that they are telling the truth and he is not?

Even if Mike is lying and he did do it, the school officials are responsible for proper supervision. The carving occurred during schooltime on school grounds. Proper supervision would have prevented extensive damage and kept the infraction a minor one. Also, the school officials had neither warned students about the penalties for defacing school property, nor had they set out standards for the type of conduct that merited suspension. But even if proper supervision and adequate warnings existed, school officials did not provide for a hearing on Michael's individual case to review the propriety of the suspension.

And, assuming that all these procedures were followed, minor property damage is not a serious enough offense to warrant a suspension. Michael represents no danger to the safety of people at school or the security of the property. School officials can very easily take steps to correct Michael's behavior without depriving him of education. They can also easily ensure the adequate supervision that would prevent a recurrence.

Even if it were a serious offense, school officials should be concerned primarily for Mike's welfare and development in school. A suspension would cause him to fall behind in his work and perhaps flunk his subjects. His promise may be lost, and his punishment may lead to more serious problems as his ties to school slip away. School officials should emphasize their first responsibility as substitute parent rather than their role as police officer.

Even if we assume that Michael can keep up with his schoolwork during a suspension, he should continue in school anyway. His action was not malicious but the result of extenuating circumstances—problems at home, peer pressure, being jilted by his girl friend, the death of his pet duck.

In addition, the vandalism represents the first time Mike has been in any trouble. There has been no pattern of disobedience that makes it likely he will step out of line again. On the contrary, his record leads to the opposite conclusion. Because this is an isolated incident, we can anticipate the future cooperation his record promises.

Besides, the guidance counselor acted improperly in extracting the admission from Michael. The counselor took advantage of a confidence after applying an overbearing psychological pressure on the boy within a confidential relationship. As a result, Michael's personal integrity and privacy rights were ignored. Michael was not advised of the serious consequences he faced.

Finally, if all else fails, you reassure them that Michael recognizes that what he did was wrong. He will benefit from the experience even without the imposition of the suspension. Mike has learned his lesson, and further punishment would only serve as a form of retribution. You tell the school officials that you know they are not interested only in revenge. You are confident that their fairness and good hearts will find sympathy for Michael and resolve this misunderstanding in his favor for his welfare.

Depending on how finely you divide, there are between twelve and fourteen separate arguments presented on Michael's behalf in this example. The key words in understanding alternative arguments are "even if." In a confrontation you fashion a number of obstacles that protect you from your adversary. Even if one argument is rejected, you can present several others that may prove successful.

Let us use the example of a showdown at high noon between two gunfighters. The rules are simple and understood by each: If Bart draws first, he plugs Billy. If Billy draws first, he plugs Bart. But suppose Bart has learned to argue in the alternative. If he draws first, he still plugs Billy. If Billy gets the drop on Bart, Bart would help his cause if he had a few alternative arguments handy. Even though you drew first, you shouldn't shoot me because you've already proven your point by outdrawing me. Even if you shoot me, the sheriff will probably hang you. Even if the sheriff doesn't hang you, my gang will track you down and bushwhack you. And so on.

Each successive step gives Bart an added chance to preserve his hide. Each additional argument you can put forward increases your chances of winning your point. So begin to think of those two powerful words, "even if," when you analyze a problem and need to construct an argument.

The principle of argument in the alternative appears as a theme with two variations. The theme is the gathering of all the available different arguments on a question for use one after the other instead of relying on one or some arguments. One variation employs different expressions of the same argument to enlist the persuasive power of repetition. The other variation resembles a tactical retreat and aims for the best results at the beginning with progressive modifications leading to a fallback position.

First, let us look at the theme itself. Your job is to gather all of the arguments that might be effective. You should allow your critical faculty to relax at first and include every idea that appears worthwhile. Approach the problem from different angles. Once you have compiled your arguments, you can see how they fit together. Now delete those that seem weak.

Often, a pattern emerges from the material. Perhaps your sense of language will lead you to a certain organization of the arguments. But even when no pattern is evident, put your strongest argument first and follow with the rest of the arguments in order of their strength. Reserve one solid argument for the conclusion. Research has shown that the positions of emphasis are the first and the last. The opening argument shapes the initial impression you make on the listener which will be carried through your entire presentation. While the opening argument sets the tone of your presentation, the last argument lingers in your listener's mind because no further ideas interfere with its reception. Put your strength at the beginning and the end.

Another practical approach involves your emotional relationship with the listener. Generally, you should start out being polite and considerate, as there may be no need to alienate the listener at all. If it becomes necessary to get tough or unpleasant, there is always time for that. Arguing alternatively includes changes in your emotional posture. Polite and friendly might lead to polite and firm, then to firm and distant, and so on, to downright nasty. Once you have been nasty, reversing the progression and becoming considerate would not produce much effect.

Derived from the idea of arguing in the alternative is the variation of a single argument through repetition. Repeating a strong argument is more important than stating every supporting argument regardless of persuasive power. Repetition can mean either an exact restatement of an argument or a different expression of the same idea. Both types of repetition work well.

If the repetition consists of an exact restatement of the argument in its same form, the optimum number of repetitions for the sake of impact and brevity is three. Three utterances give your message the best chance of sinking in and stop short of losing your listener's interest. By repeating your argument, you tell the listener to pay special attention to that part of your message because you consider it important. You also regain that percentage of your listeners whose attention wandered when you first made the statement or those who did not follow your argument fully.

More subtle, and just as important, is the format that delivers the same message but says it in a slightly different way each time. You might lose some of the driving force of the exact restatement approach, but you do not run the risk of boring your audience into inattention because they have heard it all before. Altering the style of your argument convinces a greater portion of your audience. It also increases the chances of your convincing one person head to head. One type of appeal may succeed when several others go unheeded.

Repetition stands second in importance only to an interesting style for getting your point across. Notice how often the name of a product or a feature recurs in commercials. Notice the number of times the main point crops up. Many ads purposely bludgeon you with the name of a product or a feature just to get you to remember it even though the advertisers know the ad will annoy or insult you. You must absorb and retain the argument before you can succumb to it.

After you have spent a lot of time constructing your argument, you are thoroughly familiar with it and will have no trouble remembering its key points. You may hesitate to repeat ideas that seem so obvious and comfortable, but your listeners may have heard none of them before. Whereas the first hearing exposes them to your argument, the second and third hearings bring the message home. Listeners become comfortable with the message and their minds work with yours as you restate the arguments. You have heightened both their ability to retain the message and your ability to convince them of its value.

Evidence of the effectiveness of repetition can be amazing. Even when the information is false or defies common sense, repetition can still drive home the message. Propagandists, who have established the power of repetition, call the device the "big lie." Repeat something, almost anything, often enough with authority, and people will believe it. With the increasing complexity of life in a technological world, the validity of this claim, for good or ill, will not lessen.

Up to this point, we have seen the importance of arguing alternatively so that every reason supporting your position gets an opportunity to win your case. We have seen the variation of this principle as it applies to a single argument—the value of repetition. Another variation of the principle of alternative argument concerns your reach as an advocate. It is not only permissible for your reach to exceed your grasp, but it is recommended. You should not aim for what you will settle for. Your goal lies at the farthest reaches of rationality, and you shoot for the most favorable outcome that you can support with credible evidence. Reach as high as you can for the stars without suffering an immediate pratfall in the mud.

When lawyers take negligence cases, do they sue for the amount of damages that the injury is worth or for how much they think that a jury would award? Neither. They plug in the adding machine and, with a sympathetic bleeding heart attitude, set it whirring for every imaginable dollar. Lawyers have a word that describes the arguments that result from this ambitious approach: *colorable.* Colorable means possible, believable, or worthy of consideration. It is an apt phrase, because a lot of coloring goes into a colorable argument.

Again, the second variation on the theme of alternative argument is the assertion of your strongest position at the beginning with successive modifications according to the strength of the resistance until you reach your fallback position. Your fallback position is the least favorable outcome that will still satisfy you. It corresponds to the final offer in negotiations. It is the point at which you resolve to stand firm and slug it out toe to toe.

You should attempt to define your fallback position before you even begin your arguments. This will provide structure to your case. It will also alert you to the timing of your arguments as you modify your position. As you draw near the fallback position, you should begin to concede ground more grudgingly and press your case more firmly.

If you seek only what you deserve or what you think you can get, you will probably end up settling for less. You will rarely get more than you ask for initially. More often you will surprise yourself with how much better a result turns out for you compared to what you are entitled to or what you are prepared to settle for when you present your strongest supportable case first and soften it with alternative arguments.

Our fellow Americans have a deep respect for the idea of compromise. It forms a part of the American heritage of unquestioned myths. We admire the healthy give and take of clashing viewpoints, just as we admire the contestants' sense of competition and fair play as they fashion a mutually satisfactory settlement from some middle ground. One of our most revered political figures, Henry Clay, earned the title the Great Compromiser. Our schoolchildren study the valued role of compromise in the formation of our nation from the Continental Congress and in the building of our nation in the nineteenth century.

You may accept or reject the effectiveness of compromise to act as an additional force in support of your position. The lack of military strength, for example, reduces diplomacy to an idle exercise. But, when the approximate strength of the competing interests balances, the use of compromise as an operating principle becomes indispensable. You can also draw on your opponents' respect for the compromise myth by appealing to their admiration for it. Explain that neither one of you should be unreasonable enough to insist on your original demands. You want to negotiate a compromise in which both parties give ground—and you wind up with what you were after.

Defensively, you can employ progressive alternative arguments as a holding action. Your fallback position in this case becomes what you want to prevent. You then set up advance positions from which you can offer resistance and retreat if necessary.

When you are arguing against something, you should always be ready to propose an alternative course or courses of action to handle the disadvantages and weaknesses of your position. You want to give an arbiter the easiest way out possible. He or she does not want to be forced into making a hard decision and you do not want to put him or her in that corner either. Without alternatives, you may appear to be taking an all-or-nothing stand, which comes up nothing a painful percentage of the time.

The law has a long tradition in alternative argument. In fact, the tactic is so well established in courtrooms that lawyers barely notice its operation. The laws of most states permit lawyers to plead in the alternative even when the arguments are inconsistent with each other. The judge accepts without a pause the shifting emphases and conflicting arguments of each attorney as the client's case is presented. No one should appear inconsistent in argument as a general practice. But it is important to underline the effectiveness of adopting different stances. Listeners both prefer variety in style and respond to variety in subject matter. Mixing arguments on one point based on logic, emotion, and the listener's self-interest with arguments on other points that appeal to the listener in these same varied ways remains the surest method.

This method does not violate logic, either, as logic does not concern itself with the truth or falsity of the premises or conclusions of an argument but assures that the argument itself is internally consistent and correct. You can construct an impressive syllogism that is logically correct yet as false as a three-dollar bill.

For example, apples are red; this piece of fruit is green; this piece of fruit is not an apple. A recent popular song said: "God didn't make the little green apples. . ." Our logic supports that statement, but our experience can observe apples of yellow and green as well as red.

The syllogism is logically correct. The flaw resides in the first premise. "Apples are red" is true as a generality. Some, even most, apples are red. The statement fails as a universal, however, because all apples are not red. If listeners equate the universal "all apples" with the generality "apples are red," they are ripe for plucking since their analysis is not exacting enough.

It is helpful, but not essential, that your arguments be internally consistent. You reduce your range of options if you require logical consistency among your arguments. You face too difficult a task when you require logical consistency among several arguments when the purposes of your presentations range from convincing or motivating to confusing or intimidating.

Keep your options open. This contemporary phrase deserves its popularity. The evolutionary struggle for survival has unerringly rewarded adaptability and flexibility. The Pentagon has a contingency plan for every eventuality and the size of its budget reflects the state of its health. The martial arts teach you to roll with the punches and use your opponent's thrust to your advantage. The "martial art" of advocacy responds to the same principles. Arguing alternatively represents the way the advocate protects every available option. Arguing alternatively encourages the advocate to remain flexible and to adapt his or her posture to the circumstances presented.

In short, arguing alternatively will pay its way for you many times over for these reasons:

1. Listeners respond to different appeals. Offering several arguments in different ways increases the likelihood that you will convince the listener of your position.

2. Offering several arguments increases your adversary's burden in attacking your case. A more varied approach may confuse adversaries and lead them to mistakes of omission or emphasis. You can point out arguments which they did not respond to or accent those points where they offered weak resistance.

3. You will maximize your return when you begin with your strongest colorable case and modify your position as resistance surfaces. Our trading tendencies reject another's first position and search for compromise.

Arguing in the alternative affords you an opportunity you cannot afford to miss.

Chapter 5

If You Are Going to Play the Game, Learn the Rules

Anyone who acts as his own attorney has a fool for a client.
—Lawyers' adage

Imagine for a moment a cultural exchange of unusual proportions. Take an adult living in any one of thousands of American cities, suburbs, or towns, and take an Indian dwelling in the trackless jungle of the interior Amazon. Without an introduction or explanation, magically pluck them from their homeland and place them in each other's environment—a rather cruel experiment for these unfortunates.

Imagine the American stalking food or traversing the jungles and rivers. Picture the Brazilian in a supermarket or behind the wheel of a car. You would be hard pressed to find anyone making book on the self-sufficiency, not to mention the survival, of these strangers in a strange land. They should feel fortunate that they are only products of your imagination.

This mental exercise dramatizes our dependence on the countless "rules" of everyday life that we have mastered and take for granted. We learn these rules from infancy through a continuous process of adaption. For this reason, we respect experience and bow to its judgment.

Representing ourselves in an area of specialization like the law runs contrary to this reason. Specialization implies distinct, special rules. Lawyers are naturally suspect; being tricky is part of their job. We suspect the lawyers' motive when they tell us we would be foolish to undertake some legal matter without their assistance. Perhaps we have had an unpleasant experience with a lawyer and think we could do no worse if we represented ourselves. The sad truth is that we could probably do no better.

It is not because we are not smart enough, or careful enough, or devious enough, but because we lack the training in the mechanics of the legal process. We would overlook the proper approach to a problem that legal training gives. In other words, we have not been steeped in the legal mumbo-jumbo and would miss the point of the proceeding. The same barriers would block us from successful witch doctoring or football coaching. Unless we learn the special rules, we play at a disadvantage.

For example, in some circumstances your silence can be construed as an admission, which can solidify a case against you. In other circumstances, you have a right to remain silent which is guaranteed by the U.S. Constitution. Unless you are familiar with the specific rules, such inconsistencies can create major headaches for you. The right to remain silent safeguards your right against compulsory self-incrimination in criminal law. However, in noncriminal, or civil, law, when someone says something especially damaging about you in your presence and you remain silent, a court can infer that the statement is true if it finds that an ordinary reasonable person would speak up and deny the statement. In one case silence protects you, and in the other it is your undoing.

Although they pale by comparison with doctors, lawyers still have carved out an enviable monopoly for themselves. This monopoly rests on their manufacture of special rules. Lawyers are responsible for the bulk of the laws and regulations enacted in our society. Rest assured that those regulations do not treat the lawyers too harshly. Lawyers dominate the legislatures and executive agencies as well as their private preserve—the judiciary.

Lawyers get paid to churn out, interpret, and argue about regulations. They want us to feel we are getting our money's worth. Regulations are amended and overlaid on each other until the sheer complexity strains even the drafters' understanding. Then the cry is to reform, and the rickety edifice is dismantled, only to be built anew. Lawyers, like bureaucrats, are self-feeding and self-perpetuating organisms—weeds, no doubt, to judge by their rate of growth. Lawyers are proudest when their work on a problem or project spawns several other problems. Like doting grand-parents, they watch their offspring multiply.

Our dependence on lawyers results from all of this breeding and building. Because of studies, associations, and experience, lawyers are familiar with the formal and informal procedures that govern a legal matter. They can argue effectively in court because they recognize hearsay and know how to lay the foundation for the admission of evidence. They can represent a buyer of real estate because they know what defects will cloud good title to the property and how those defects can be corrected.

If a legal matter falls outside of the area of competence of one lawyer, the case might be referred to another lawyer with expertise in that area or, at least, the original lawyer will research the law and consult with colleagues so that he or she can handle the case competently. Most lawyers would plunge into an unfamiliar area with their ignorance intact about as quickly as they would leave the house naked in the morning. To act without acquiring the knowledge to act competently invites a serious malpractice suit.

Likewise, before you proceed with any activity that involves significant consequences, check yourself out on the rules. Do you know how the game is played? Do you know what you are playing for? If the name of the game is the battle of the bazookas from ten paces, you are allowed fewer mistakes and fewer scores by your opponent than if you were playing table tennis. Nor can you afford to be as gracious in bazookas at ten paces as in letting your opponent serve first in table tennis. You also may reject the plan of waiting until your opponent's ammunition is spent before charg-ing his or her position if the game uses bazookas.

The idea of this chapter is that you must master the rules of the game beforehand in order to play the game most effectively. Preparedness and familiarity anchor the message. Prepare for the situation you face by becoming familiar with the rules that govern it. In other words, avoid on-the-job training. Planning is superior to improvisation. Only when you have mastered the operative principles of your task can you formulate a planned course of action. Without this basis, you may scramble or stumble through to your objective. But it is not as likely and harder on the nerves.

In order to illustrate the point, let us return to the law. After examining some of the rules there, we can explore some practical rules that will apply in many advocacy situations.

The law has three levels of rules: procedure, substance, and policy. Procedure channels the argument into an understandable structure. Procedural rules govern the mechanics of the case, the form—the way things should be done. They provide the format for the argument and usually remain extraneous to its resolution: they outline how long a pleading can be, the deadline for filing it, and who must receive it. They also determine which court to go to, how to get others who are involved in the case to appear, and how they should testify.

Except for the recent popularity of law school clinics, law schools have not taught procedure. Lawyers learn procedure from experienced lawyers they work under or with, from continuing education seminars, or from their research in law libraries among formbooks and handbooks. Law schools take the position that they must emphasize substantive law and the proper approach to legal problems rather than often temporary rules that can be learned easily. Procedure often changes from one locality to another and much of it is unwritten and the product of custom.

Substantive rules comprise what the average person thinks of as the law. Laws enacted by the legislature, the body of previous court decisions on a certain topic, the Constitution as interpreted by the Supreme Court, administrative regulations, and city ordinances all fit into the category of substantive law. Let us be more specific so you get a flavor of the substance of law: murder, theft, conspiracy and their punishments; the grounds for getting a divorce; no taking of private property for a public purpose without adequate compensation; traffic laws; negligence actions because of personal injury or property damage; and inheritance laws.

The law presumes that we know and understand the hundreds of thousands of rules that affect our lives. Normally we do not suffer because of this presumption. Certainly ignorance is bliss when compared with the pursuit of this staid knowledge in any depth. The substantive law is the source of authority that a judge turns to, and ideally follows, when deciding a dispute.

The third level of rules is the policy level. Policy seeks to carry out the purpose of the law. Policy represents the underlying assumptions at the foundation of the system. The policy level has two parts. One corresponds to the positive side of human nature and is readily articulated. The other part represents the darker side of human nature and is rarely articulated; only slightly more often are we even aware of it.

To unearth the policy considerations, let us look at torts, which are personal injuries generally remedied by civil, rather than criminal, law. Tort law attempts to reconcile two fundamental interests and human needs—activity and security. One person's unrestricted activity will hamper another's security. The right to bear arms does not include the vigilante's solution of eradicating presumed criminals. Full protection of one person's security will impede another's legitimate activity. What constitutes a harmless expression of free speech for one may seem like disturbing the peace to another.

Tort law resolves the clash of these two desirable interests— activity and security—in individual disputes. The positive policy behind tort law is to preserve both of these competing interests. The law balances the benefit of the activity to the actor (and to society) with the risk of harm to those in the zone of the activity (and to society).

The catchword in torts is "reasonableness." The actor's conduct must conform to the basic standard of the "ordinary reasonable person." Would an ordinary reasonable person foresee the risk of harm his or her activities create?

Intention is relevant but assumes less importance than it has in criminal law. Actors without malice or moral blame can still be liable for what they should have known or foreseen, because they have the duty to others to avoid unreasonable risks of harm. The law inquires into causation but avoids philosophical distinctions. Causation works to limit the liability of the actor by establishing how remote the injury is from the activity that caused it. If the injury is unreasonably remote from the activity, then the actor did not cause the injury and is not liable for it. Reasonableness rules.

The other, darker side of policy which is rarely articulated reflects the elemental function of tort law, indeed all law, as a means of social control. The powerful use the law to retain their influence, while the wealthy use the law to safeguard their property. The law keeps the have-nots separated from the haves. The best the have-nots can hope for is enlightened despotism from a sympathetic judge or socially conscious lawyer. The conformity, education, and resources of those who make and interpret the law alienate them from society's outsiders and disadvantaged. Legal decisions emanate from the solid, respectable, and conservative segment of society.

The tort law of libel and slander compensates for injury to reputation when it results in a loss of money. The plaintiff must prove money damages at the outset to prevent the court from dismissing a negligence case before even hearing from the defense. Trespass and nuisance actions secure the landholder. So it helps to have money or property to begin with. Tort law staunchly defends the entrenched economic interests. Tort law guards the status quo, resisting change regardless of its merit. Only when society has incorporated change through other means will the law neatly pirouette to adapt to the now acceptable new standard.

This analysis of the law has ranged from procedure to substance to policy. The discussion exemplifies the depth your preparation should attain as you become familiar with your subject. Uncover the layers of fact beneath the surface of apparent fact. Before you are ready for action, understand the rules that preside over the activity.

Suppose you are applying for a job. Find out who really has the power to hire you instead of submitting yourself to the vagaries of the personnel office. Find out what skills the employer seeks instead of simply listing your abilities in the abstract. Show the employer that there are benefits to be gained from your services instead of asking about the fringe benefits you would receive. Find out if your ability will determine if you get the job or if political clout or personal connections are the controlling factors in the selection process.

Does it almost kill you to see the high cost of dying? If you still decide to go through with your death eventually, knowledge of one simple rule will enable you to beat the exorbitance of the rigged burial game. Take comfort in the fact that the U.S. Navy will bury you at sea for no charge. The ship will neither stray from its scheduled course nor can the Navy assure you that it will even slow down, but that should not cause any further discomfort. If you have already made enough of a splash during your life, many states have rules that allow the deceased's ashes to be scattered over a body of water from the air, resulting in great savings compared to more conventional methods. No one outlasts the Grim Reaper, but familiarity with the rules can ease your introduction. The point of the example is that even in death we do not have a refuge from the influence of rules.

At this point let us consider some of the practical rules that pertain to the two functions of the advocate—argument and persuasion. If you are going to play the game, learn the rules. Since advocacy is the name of the game you will be playing so frequently, these rules should help considerably.

To simplify the rules of argument, let us divide them into three topics: strategy, structure, and emphasis. When your opponent has advanced a contention, you must choose a strategy to follow in your response. Depending on the circumstances, one of several approaches could produce the most telling effect.

First, you can assert that the opponent's contention is irrelevant. You must show that what is said does not relate to the subject of the argument or that, although it relates to the subject, it does not support the position your opponent has taken. In other words, it is true, but so what?

Second, you can attack the truth of the contention. Assess the evidence your adversary uses to support the contention. Where is it false or weak? Has only one side of the story been told, and has evidence favorable to your point of view been omitted? Attack the opposing evidence where it is wrong or weak, and offer whatever additional evidence you can muster that refutes your opponent's contention.

Third, while accepting your opponent's contention as true, challenge the significance of the point being made. Another "so what?" posture results as when you charge irrelevancy. You concede the truth of the statement but insist the statement is not important. The judge should weigh the statement slightly, if at all, in arriving at a decision.

Fourth, you accept the contention; you accept its importance; then you offer a contention of your own and argue that your counterproposal has greater importance. This greater importance overrides the value of your adversary's contention.

Fifth, you co-opt your opponent's position by taking the evidence presented in support of the opposing contention, and show that the evidence actually substantiates your contention.

You need not limit yourself to choosing one of these five strategies and excluding the rest. Bear in mind the value of alternative argument. As long as you maintain the clarity of your presentation and emphasize your strongest points, you can use several of the strategies at the same time.

How should you organize your presentation in order to drive your message through most effectively? Build on this five-point structure:

1. State your opponent's argument in your own words. Express this argument in a way that benefits your view, but remain fair to its substance. You are not attacking it yet; you are restating it succinctly. Use more than one sentence only if it is absolutely necessary.

2. Characterize your opponent's argument and identify its weakness. For example: "This is a faulty analogy." "This statement is true as far as it goes, but it leaves out several important facts." "Contrary facts show that this statement assumes too much." "My opponent confuses cause and effect."

3. State your argument simply, directly, and slowly. State it dramatically. Perhaps state it more than once. You want very much to leave a permanent impression on the judge.

4. Support your argument with the evidence you have gathered.

5. Conclude with a summary of your argument. Restate the essence of your argument, comment on its importance or validity, or wrap up your presentation with an unifying idea or example. In short, put the pieces together so that you can close with a punch. The impact of your summary should jar the judge's mind and reverberate after you have finished.

You can devise the necessary variations on this structure to suit the circumstances. On occasion, you may want to start with an example or begin by characterizing your adversary's argument immediately. Some alteration of the structure may fit your personal style better.

The last set of rules concerning argument relates to emphasis. Necessity forces you to stress some points at the expense of others. How do you choose the parts of your argument that you will rely on?

First, emphasize your strengths rather than correcting or explaining away your weaknesses. Stay on the offensive by hammering away at your strongest arguments. When you have your opponents reacting to your case instead of arguing their own, you have earned the greatest advantage.

Second, pay close attention and put the most effort into responding to your opponent's strongest arguments. You must meet these arguments in some fashion, even if it is with distraction, and neutralize their influence. Offering no resistance makes a strong argument seem stronger. If you do not rebut a strong argument, it will leave a lasting impression on the judge. When you cannot offer contrary evidence or argument, try to confuse the issue or shift the ground of the argument. Usually, distraction works best when you are outgunned and have little to lose by trying a ploy. Respond as best you can, but respond.

Third, spend more time on what your adversary has spent the most time on or already emphasized. Without other indications to guide your emphasis, you can assume that your opponent will spend the most time on the important parts of the opposing case. If your assumption is wrong, you are in a better position nonetheless because your adversary is arguing inefficiently and probably ineffectively.

We have seen some rules of argument from the standpoint of strategy, structure, and emphasis. Now let us turn to the other function of the advocate and outline some of the rules which underlie persuasion.

The techniques of persuasion encompass too much ground to be covered in a few paragraphs. Whole books have been devoted to the subject. This book weaves devices of persuasion throughout the text. One of this book's major themes consists of explaining the methods and skills that persuade another of your viewpoint. So for now let us just sketch the rules of a basic approach. These rules can be used as a starting point to help you focus on the problem at hand and act as a springboard to the other devices you will find elsewhere in the book.

The rules are: know your audience, know your purpose, and know your method. The more closely you can identify with your audience and present your message in their language, the more receptive the audience will be and the more likely it is that the audience will accept your message. Spend the time to study the makeup of the audience. How large and cohesive is the audience? What brought it together? What is the mood? What are the age and sex of the audience? What are the occupations and educational levels? What are the attitudes, opinions, and beliefs the audience brings to your subject? What is the ethnic, economic, and cultural background? What are the desires, prejudices, special interests, and life experiences? What does the audience know about you and your message? What is their probable response?

Apply these questions to an individual as well as a group. Develop your own amateur psychological profile of your audience. Once you know your audience, you will know the ways and means that have the best prospect of persuading the audience.

The second rule requires you to examine the purpose of your persuasion. Do you want to convince the audience of the truth of your position or the falsity of another position? Do you want to incite your audience to initiate some action? Do you want to stimulate the audience to consider certain issues? The purpose you have in mind subtly influences the persuasion devices you select. If you seek to incite to a momentary action rather than to convince an audience for a long period of time, your techniques would probably be more direct, inflammatory, emotional, and shallow.

Finally, know your method. If you have identified your audience and your purpose, choosing the most effective method should naturally flow from your other efforts. The method consists of your style; the devices you employ such as repetition, rationalization, and the two-valued orientation; and how you mix them together.

Suppose your study of the audience has shown that it is made up of educated, cohesive adults, unimpressed by you, and disrespectful of your subject. Suppose that your purpose is to stimulate. Generally, your style should be low-key and indirect. You should rely heavily on external forms of persuasion and play down your own role and visibility. Since the audience does not respect the subject, you should call on emotional appeals more heavily than on logic. Rationalize more, assert less. Combining logical and emotional appeals is more effective than relying on one or the other, but the circumstances should lead you to stress one over the other.

We often hear the phrase "Know your rights." To know your rights is to learn the rules that affect you in a formal or legal sense. Why stop there? Let us follow through. Know your rules. Learn all the rules that affect the significant actions of your life. Knowledge is power. When you understand the forces that govern your actions, you are prepared to influence those forces for your benefit. You can manage your own life. You will get the feeling that you control what happens to you. And that is a very nice feeling.

Chapter 6

Law versus Equity: Principles versus Sympathy

Law has the practical function of adjusting everyday relations so as to meet current ideas of fair play.

—*Ezra Pound*

Peel a bureaucrat and you will find the insides wrapped tighter than a golf ball with red tape. The bureaucrat is an unsympathetic sort who would cancel attendance at a father-son banquet because it violates sexual equality. He will reject a suggestion on how to economize because it was not submitted in triplicate—with an extra copy for the files. The most noble and heartrending plea will fall on deaf ears because his function does not include that area of responsibility; he can show you his job description to prove it.

Bureaucrats do not lack principles. This is a case of principles running amok untempered by the balm of sympathy. The absence of sympathy in a bureaucrat or anyone else makes persuasion a most difficult job. Fortunately, most people are sympathetic by nature. Even the bureaucrat, exaggerated by our caricature, actually possesses a modest amount.

Compared to our present legal system in the United States, the common law of England of several hundred years ago was rigid, unyielding, and unsympathetic. It would have put any self-respecting bureaucrat to shame. Following the rules of law produced

51

harsh results, and yet no alternative existed to settle disputes. People could not find comfort in laws that did not respond to their sense of fair play. This resulted in the emergence of a system of equity. At first people just went to the king to get a special exception from the law, but eventually a separate court system developed to hear the cases that fell between the cracks in the law.

Equity afforded an extraordinary remedy in that it acted as a safety valve in situations where the law was inadequate. Equity allowed the court to make exceptions in order to treat people fairly. The normal remedy of the law was money damages. However, some injuries did not result in a loss of money, and in others the sum of money lost could not be calculated accurately.

Equity evolved special remedies to redress the injury. Injunctions forbade a certain action by defendants. Specific performance required a certain action of them. With the remedies of rescission and reformation, the judge could cut and stitch like a surgeon to repair a faulty contract.

Today, the courts of law and equity have merged into one, and each judge in every court sits as a judge of both legal and equitable claims. One lawsuit can often include one or more claims based in both law and equity. But law and equity have different characteristics. Whereas law is fixed, intellectual, and principled, equity is flexible, emotional, and sympathetic. In other words if law is the head, then equity is the heart. The law represents stability, uniformity, and predictability, while equity represents progress, justice, and public policy.

Through the years, decisions founded on equitable considerations precipitated a number of equitable maxims. These sayings manifest the view that equity championed. Because they are generalities, they give a taste of the overall values and attitudes that concern equity. In order for you to get a sense of equity's mission, let us list the more common equitable maxims:

1. Equity acts *in personam*.* That is, equity responds to personal wrongs by enforcing its code against the transgressing individuals rather than against property.

In personam: against or concerning the person, distinguished from *in rem,* against or concerning the thing (meaning property or tangibles).

2. Equity does not suffer wrong to be without a remedy. Thus, equity can redress a wrong even though no formal remedy existed at the time of the wrong.
3. Equity follows the law. Equity fills gaps in the law but it will not contradict or undermine established rules of law.
4. Equitable remedies are discretionary. Judges are not bound to invoke equity because of a certain set of facts.
5. Where the equities are equal, the law prevails.
6. Where the equities are equal, the first in time prevails.
7. Anyone who seeks equity must do equity. One who asks for basic fairness from the court must act fairly toward others even though the law may not require one to do so.
8. Anyone who comes into equity must come with clean hands. One who has acted inequitably cannot go to the courts of equity and complain of inequitable treatment.
9. Delay defeats equity.
10. Equality is equity.
11. Equity looks to the intent and not to the form.
12. Equity regards as done that which ought to be done.

Equity focuses on the conduct of the parties more than on formal requirements. It rewards upright behavior and treats parties as if they guide their actions by positive moral standards. Where they do not act ethically, they suffer for it at the hands of the court.

Equity participates with the established precedents of law to shape the judge's decision. The common law system of precedents has been compared to a stream that changes its own banks. The moral force of equity causes most of the erosion and fixes the new directions of the stream's flow. On the one hand, there is a tendency to treat every case as another manifestation of a settled general category and apply the rules handed down from the earlier cases of that category. On the other hand, there is a tendency to treat each case as an unique problem that contains the seeds of its own solution within itself. The creative tension between law and equity preserves the divergent values of stability and flexibility.

The lawyer arguing in court sees two judges. The lawyer has not forgotten to wear glasses and did not imbibe excessively the night before; both judges are in one body. One judge is concerned with the knowledge of the rules of law from similar cases of the past. The other brings the conscience of society to the dispute between its members and strives to find the fundamentally fair resolution.

The judge sorts out the times when the rule holds sway from the times the exception upholds the rule. He or she is both a technician and a humanist. More like a painter than a photographer, the judge must perceive the landscape accurately. But he or she does not try to reproduce it exactly as in a negative. Rather, the essential truth of the subject must be captured. The materials of the artist—paints, brushes, and so on—represent society's values, and the judge's perspective which seeks that justice be done parallels the inspired vision of the painter. The judge refines society's values with a personal sense of fairness as he or she works on the canvas of the case.

Confronted with this ambivalent authority, the lawyer fashions arguments to appeal to both principles and sympathies in order to achieve maximum effect. He or she argues the equities of the case along with the rules of law. Reason and logic help construct a tight, legal argument based on precedents and relevant facts. Emotions and compassion are called on to win the favor of the judge for the plight of the client and for the client's integrity. The lawyer varies his or her approach from one to the other and back in a blend of arguments that aims to touch every responsive impulse in the judge.

The division of the law and of the lawyers' arguments into legal and equitable considerations provides a worthwhile lesson for your own advocacy. You must argue the substance of your case. Without it you have no case and no chance of winning your argument. However, you should not limit yourself to the principles or precedents that will influence the decision. Include the factors that will elicit sympathy, that will appeal to a sense of fair play, and that will stimulate an emotional identification with your situation.

Something as staid and rigid as the law developed a large independent branch like equity to carve exceptions out of the law. This branch not only endured; it thrives. It is even more valid for you to develop an equitable branch of arguments in your dealings in less formal spheres.

The prosperity of equity reminds us that the rules governing our case are only the starting point in our presentation. We are human beings, not computers, in that we have feelings as well as thoughts. And in most of us our feelings predominate over our intellects. Certainly, in persuasion we court the feelings harder than the intellect.

Experts in persuasion have discerned three dimensions to an argument: truth, value, and significance. The experts rate value as the strongest part of the argument followed by truth and significance. Truth and significance correspond to the legal weight of an argument, while value is analogous to the equitable considerations. If those who have studied persuasion scientifically were to apply their findings to the legal-equitable distinction, they would select the equitable appeal as the dominant one. While the legal case is the more necessary, the equitable case is the more effective.

Our culture sympathizes with the underdog. It is to your advantage to find a slant to your presentation that portrays you as the little guy fighting to defend a just cause. When the rules point the other way or the standard operating procedure blocks you, look for an interpretation that establishes you as a worthy case for an exception to the routine. Show your judge that to blindly follow the beaten path of a policy in your case would frustrate the purpose of the policy and lead to an unfair and undesirable result.

Several persuasive devices can help you in putting together an argument that will evoke your audience's sympathy. In identification, one of these devices, you match your presentation to the characteristics, attitudes, and beliefs of the audience. The more you seem to be one of them, the more attention they will give to what you say and the more readily they will agree to what you want.

Politicians are diligent practitioners of this device of identification. They step out of the bastions of wealth and privilege and undergo a drastic transformation to appear as average persons, just ordinary citizens like you and me. As the election draws near, they abandon paneled offices and exclusive clubs, traveling from shopping centers to civic groups with rolled-up sleeves and idiomatic speech patterns. They claim to be worthy of support because they are of the people. Politicians win votes and continued access to enclaves of privilege because of their ability to identify with the voter, to blend in with popular sentiments, and to project themselves as representatives of the masses.

A slight twist of tactics in the use of identification preys on the herd instinct. Instead of identifying with your audience, you encourage your audience to identify with your message. You portray your message as "with it," the "in" thing to do. No one wants to be behind the times or "out of it." Everyone wants to belong. You can satisfy that desire to be a part of the action by letting your audience know that everyone who counts thinks this way or does this. It is hard to resist the impulse to follow the crowd.

Another persuasive device that gains you the sympathy of your audience is rationalization. (We have seen something of this device already.) Rationalization, a substitute for reasoning, is a form of self-deception that produces reasons and logic to support a position already arrived at irrationally. People do not like to admit they hold a certain belief or act a certain way because of selfish motives, weaknesses, or emotions. Your job is to supply your audience with the rational structure of altruistic reasons and admirable motives that warrant the belief or action. Your rationalization lays the groundwork of respectability that enables the audience to justify their positions and feel good about them.

If the audience thinks your prestige or expertise is minimal, you can encourage the audience to rationalize. By supplying the raw materials of opinions, knowledge, and examples that the audience already holds or that build on what the audience already believes, you allow the audience to avail themselves of this rational basis to wrap their positions in respectability through their own rationalization process.

An example of rationalization might occur when you buy some new clothes that you do not need and cannot afford. The reasons you buy are because the clothes make you look sexy, you feel good wearing them, and you just love to shop for clothes. Rationalization eases you out of your guilt. You tell yourself, or the salesperson tells you, that the clothes will be an asset to you in your job, that they will last longer, that they cost less to clean, and that they are on sale.

Finally, you can use distraction in calling upon sympathy to overcome a nettlesome rule. Distraction ignores relevancy. Leaving aside the subject at hand, distraction meanders in search of any stories, exhortations, or pleas that curry enough favor with the audience so that the members do not notice, or do not mind, the shift in the discussion. Distraction says we know that there are rules but they are no fun; let us turn our attention to something more interesting instead. Distraction is the flirt who tells us there is plenty of time for business later.

Under the doctrine in the law called equitable conversion, the risk of loss in a transaction shifts from the seller to the buyer when the contract for sale is entered into, even though title passes to the buyer at a later time. Besides being another example of equity's intercession in the law, this doctrine provides a nice phrase to help us remember the important aid to effective argument presented in this chapter. Use the words *equitable conversion* as a reminder to you of the added breadth of your argument. You have undergone an equitable conversion. You have converted to equitable argument. You need not religiously develop a new consciousness for this conversion. Just remember to include and emphasize overtures to sympathy or fair play along with the technical basis of principles or rules in the presentation of your case.

Chapter 7

Simple and Direct

I should be glad if I could flatter myself that I came as near to the central idea of the occasion in two hours, as you did in two minutes.

—*Edward Everett, to Abe Lincoln*

Edward Everett, a famous orator of the last century, spoke at Gettysburg for two hours before Lincoln presented his brief address. What did Everett say? No one remembers.

This chapter considers the problem of getting your message through to your audience and will provide a simple structure to accomplish that end.

Several formidable obstacles seem to block the way; for example, the attention span of most people is shockingly short. Often people will not be listening at all to what you say. Those who do listen often receive only the impulses from their senses; they do not digest the meaning those impulses convey. They hear, but they do not discern. When your audience gets your message, you have no assurance that they will retain it long enough for it to do any good.

These people are not jaded or discourteous. They are exhibiting normal characteristics of human nature. Do not be put off. That same human nature, through many of the same characteristics, works in your favor. Lazy minds engage in sloppy thinking. Prejudices supplant analysis and judgment. Emotions skim over logic and reasoning. Desires of the moment destroy a balanced perspective. The same attributes that make the delivery of your message a critical concern contribute to receiving the message uncritically.

From your side of the equation, the difficulty lies in expressing your message clearly. Language likes to play tricks with what you want to say, and unless you take care to state your message simply and directly, there is a good chance the audience will receive a message different from the one you send. Communication is haphazard, chancy, imperfect, and often a distortion.

If you are aware of the shortcomings of your audience, of language, and of yourself, and if you make a concerted effort to avoid the pitfalls these shortcomings create, you will be amply rewarded. So few other messages will have arrived unscathed that your message will have scant competition. Our distracted minds offer so many obstacles that the hardy messages that run the course successfully are welcomed with respect.

Focus on two objectives: (1) you want to gain and maintain the attention of your audience, and (2) you want to make your point clearly and forcefully during the brief time you have your audience's attention. Again, the term audience includes an audience of one.

Expert opinion on attention span length varies, but it can be measured in seconds. However, it is not as important for you to know whether your audience has an attention span of ten or thirty seconds as it is for you to be eternally conscious of the short amount of time your audience will be with you.

You have longer than a few seconds in total, however, because attention comes in spurts. It wanders leisurely until it is captured, but it remains only briefly before escaping for another jaunt afield. So maintaining attention is a misnomer. You should be satisfied with regaining attention periodically during your presentation at the times you design. No one can maintain attention continuously throughout a presentation.

How can we engage the minds of our listeners when we have caught their attention? The answer is by arousing curiosity, by surprise, and by involving your audience.

You can arouse curiosity with a question or series of questions that stimulate thought. You can tell a story that introduces your point or fill in the background facts that lead to your point. You can describe a scene that lacks completion: a conflict that needs resolution, a group of effects without the cause, or a group of causes without the effect. If your approach takes on the aspects of a puzzle, you will encourage the audience to seek the solution. They will then listen to compare answers or to find out what your answer is.

The object of surprise is to give your audience a mild shock that will awaken them for your message. You can do this by what you say and by how you say it. If you plan to startle the audience by what you say, have a resolution ready in advance that will set them back at ease. You can do this by playing on a word's different meanings. But you only want to give a mild shock. For example, if you were to tell your audience the building is on fire, they would resent you for scaring them regardless of the skill of your explanation or twist.

How you say something can also startle your audience into surrendering their attention to you. You can raise your voice or lower it; change your cadence or inflection; use body movements such as waving your arms, turning to one side, hitting a table or the like; or you can pause for an extra beat or two until the silence becomes noticeable.

Involving your audience pays heed to the notion that one's favorite subject is oneself. Relate your material to the audience and their local interests. What are the main concerns of the audience? What are the current events or topics that are important to them or fascinate them? How can you arrange your material and message so that it follows and flows from the interests of the audience? When your presentation coincides with the ideas that are already on the minds of your audience, you will find that their attention will stay with you longer and return sooner when it wanders.

Flattery is a proven attention getter. You can drone on at great length until your audience yawns and nods. But throw in a solid, sincere compliment, and they will be right back with you.

Involving the audience can also mean giving the audience an

actual role in the proceedings. Adopting a question-and-answer format under your direction provides variety and animation. Asking the audience to do something like a show of hands makes them feel a part of what is going on.

In all of the methods used to involve the audience, the objective is to convert the audience from spectator to participant, and from passive receptor to active contributor. When you watch the action from the removed position of the spectator, you know that you can drift off easily and the action will be there when you come back; therefore no concentration is required. But as a participant, your concentration remains with the action.

Once you have gained or regained that precious commodity, the attention of the audience, you must make the most of the few seconds allotted before attention sneaks away again. Remember to be direct and to keep it simple.

Get to the point. Your audience will love you for it and bend over backwards to accept what you say. Those who can make their point concisely gain respect that carries over to their message. No one is more exasperating than persons who talk around and around a subject without saying what they came to say. They are like an itch that will not go away, and the audience becomes restless, then irritated.

Have you ever run into someone whose stories pile mountains of irrelevant detail upon a bona fide one-liner? The marathon narration is always punctuated with, "To make a long story short. . .," every so often only to tease you. When you can find no avenue of escape, you silently plead to be put out of your misery. You think it must end sometime, but your doubts obliterate any comfort you may take from that hope. You resent that sadist so much that you begin not to care what is said.

Even if we accept the improbable assumption that we have so much to say that we could speak productively for a long time, we still face the limitation of the attention span. Your audience cannot absorb all of the gems you are ready to bestow on them. Do not try to prove more than is necessary, as you would probably confuse the issue and wind up with less.

Pick the most precious. Cut and polish until the core shines brilliantly. A direct statement of your message is your crowning jewel.

Studies on persuasion and suggestion confirm the importance of stating your message directly. Opinion change in an audience generally results when the conclusion of the speaker is explicitly stated. Suggesting a desired response directly is more effective than arguing against a response that is opposed. A negative approach tends to defeat itself.

Getting to the point directly implies its twin obligation—simplicity. What you say should be simple enough so that you have no doubt the audience understands your point. Have you ever heard someone make a complicated assertion and follow it with, "What I mean to say. . . " or "In other words. . ."? If you say what you mean at the beginning, you will not seem like a muddled apologist for your point of view. If you are not before the Supreme Court, leave aside formalism and pretentious language, and use plain words that will not stand in the way of your meaning.

The strongest exhibit for the effectiveness of a simple, direct message is the slogan. Slogans are short, simple, and make a single point. They catch our attention and fix themselves in our minds. Do you remember the policies and programs Eisenhower espoused, or do you remember "I like Ike"? Those three words captured the essence of Eisenhower's appeal to the country—comfortable, secure, grandfatherly, informal. Advertising slogans bouncing around in our heads could be the trait that identifies Americans most closely. Their insidious presence verifies how well they work. In communication, less is more.

The best structure you can follow in order to get your message through simply and directly is to tell what you are going to tell; tell it; and tell what you told.

We have already seen the power of repetition and know that the greatest impact occurs when a message is delivered three times. Our structure harnesses the power of triple expression. Make sure, however, that each expression varies somewhat in form, style, and delivery.

First, introduce the subject and pique the interest of the audience. Tell what you are going to tell. Next, deliver the body of information comprising your subject. Tell it. Last, review the message you have left in a summation to solidify the audience's hold on it. Tell what you told. In practical language, prime the surface, apply the paint or stain, and varnish or wax to protect the finish.

The positions of strength for emphasis are the beginning and the end, but the middle holds the body of your subject. So you wind up with three expressions when you play to your strength even if you discount the impact of repetition itself. The different slant caused by the varied purposes of introduction, delivery, and solidification provides impetus for you to inject variety in your presentation. Variations on a constant theme produce the best results. Different manifestations of a constant message cumulate the effect. Variety keeps the message fresh while repetition is hammering it home.

A simple, direct presentation, spiced with a variety of repetitions, delivers your message most persuasively. This wisdom may not be relied upon by all after-dinner speakers, but it is not a secret formula available to a select few. Its origins lie in the books of English composition that we all studied in high school and probably have not looked at since. One text would teach clarity, brevity, and emphasis, and another, unity, emphasis, and coherence. Still another would teach economy, force, and naturalness. But whatever adjectives were selected to describe style, they sought to instill the same qualities.

Clarity, unity, and coherence contribute to making your meaning clear. Use familiar words that have a common meaning for most people. Use short sentences. Fill in background information needed for understanding, and explain again if the audience does not seem to understand. Make a special point not to distract the audience with complicated or flowery constructions, slang, or vulgarity.

Brevity and economy require the shortest presentation possible while still getting your message across. Irrelevant explanation, unnecessary elaboration, and redundancy only dilute your message.

Emphasis and force give your message punch. By using concrete, descriptive, or action words, you can take advantage of the positions of emphasis and of repetition. These are the basic points that English composition texts stress. If you suspect that your style is sometimes weak or vague, review one of these texts. There is always more to learn about effective style.

Another source for valuable lessons on style is advertising copy. Pay close attention to the ads in magazines and on television and radio. Reflect on how they are delivering the message instead of what the message is. The people who write ads are professionals and are paid for the skills of style they possess.

This chapter has discussed the importance of getting to the point directly and stating your message simply because of the fleeting attention span of the audience. A simple structure has been outlined which compensates for the difficulties of holding attention and for the imprecision of language, while it incorporates the main principles of effective style.

If you need a plan of attack, tell what you'll tell; tell it; and tell what you told. After all, if your message hasn't gotten through clearly, it doesn't matter how much preparation you have done, or how eloquent your presentation, or how worthy your subject. You can only convince someone who is listening to your argument.

Chapter 8

Discovery

Knowledge is power.

—*Thomas Hobbes*, Leviathan

"Your witness." The lawyer rises resolutely from the defense table. She approaches the apprehensive witness. The witness holds his hands tightly in his lap and steals quick glances at the lawyer. The lawyer begins her questions softly and slowly, disarming the witness with a friendly solicitude. She goes over the key points of the story the witness had told on direct examination.

Once the cross-examination has isolated those answers of the witness that may help the defense case, the lawyer begins to confront the witness. "You testified that defendant's peanut brittle stuck in your tooth at a party on April first and that was the cause of the infection. Is it not true you went to a dentist three weeks earlier complaining of this same infection which has gummed up your mouth?" The witness is now caught between a thorn and a briar. "Did you not, in fact, refuse another guest's offer of a jawbreaker less than a half-hour before, saying that you needed to watch your mouth?" The witness fidgets and mumbles. And so on.

The witness had not included the dentist and the jawbreaker in his original recital of what had happened. This was probably an unintentional oversight since, of course, the witness was under oath to tell the whole truth. Was the defendant blessed with a lawyer with highly developed intuition who sensed the whole truth? It would be too much to believe that she could make two such lucky guesses back to back about very special occurrences.

The truth is less exciting. It seems that the lawyer had discovered the facts well before the trial. She had examined her adversary's dental records. She had questioned the dentist and the other guest from the party under oath about holes in her adversary's mouth, and in his case.

Discovery in the law refers to the exchange of information that happens at the beginning stages of a lawsuit. Each side is entitled to ask its opponent for the facts which support the opponent's case and for any other relevant information. The law interprets the scope of discovery broadly. It invites the maximum exposure of each side's case to the other, in order to encourage settlements instead of costly, time-consuming trials.

A party may discover any information that is relevant to the proceedings not only from a party but from any source that is not privileged. The subpoena powers of the court can be used to gain the cooperation of an indifferent neutral party. If that neutral party does not disclose the information, the judge can impose a jail sentence until he or she has a change of heart.

The law has shaped a number of discovery devices to ease the task of gathering information from a reluctant adversary. The ones most frequently used are oral or written depositions, written interrogatories to parties, production of documents or things, physical or mental examinations, and admissions of facts.

In a deposition, prospective witnesses must answer under oath questions put to them by the opposing attorney. Written interrogatories to a party are written questions that the other party must answer under oath. Even if they do not know the answer to a question, they have a duty to search their files for information available to them. Even if they have no personal knowledge of a fact, they must tell what they know and the basis of their knowledge.

A party may request another party to produce documents or physical evidence for inspection, copying, or testing. One party may cause another party to undergo a physical or mental examination when that party's physical or mental condition is at issue in the litigation. Finally, one party may request that an adverse party admit the truth of certain facts or the genuineness of documents. The facts are presumed to be admitted unless denied or the adverse party gives reasons why the facts cannot be admitted or denied.

This brief description of the tools of discovery shows how wide their range of operation is and how much muscle they have. The only practical limits to the extent of discovery are the client's pocketbook and the attorney's perseverance. The overwhelming majority of lawsuits are won or lost before the trial begins during the time when discovery and pretrial pleadings are taking place. Piercing through your opponent's shield of evasion to learn the crucial facts and frustrating your opponent's attempts to ferret out your vulnerable facts will win your case before the trial starts.

Attorneys who would bypass the smooth and easy road of discovery for the steep and rocky road of courtroom dramatics, outwitting hostile witnesses, and impassioned pleas are either fools or masochists. They deserve what their unfortunate clients wind up getting. Why gamble on the chance that a witness might break down or a telling fact might surface when you can systematically pursue all the information you need to establish a case? Why endure a long, demanding trial when you can find out from a few questions that your case is too weak to press?

Only a few exceptional attorneys are descended from bloodhounds and Scotland Yard detectives, who, sniffing at answers, postures, and atmospheres, can smell a slight trace of fabrication and can track an admission through a tangled underbrush of explanations or a rushing stream of alibis and denials. Luck smiles on a few other attorneys who stumble upon the right path unwittingly. Longshots do come home infrequently enough to nourish our vain hopes in perpetuity. But more cases are lost than won by shooting in the dark.

For those of us who lack genius, planning and preparation rout the opportune question or the chance revelation as the preferred method of operation. Most effective cross-examinations are based on facts already discovered and not on cunning or intuition.

An accepted dictum of cross-examination warns attorneys never to ask a question for which they do not already know the answer. A probing question will lead more often to embarrassment or to the damage of your case than it will to helpful information.

What application can we make of the principles of discovery to our everyday trials? We can state the lesson in one sentence: Find out as much about the other side while revealing as little of your side as you can. While you try to learn as much of the opponent's case as possible before the crunch, you should also conceal as much of your own case and your plan of action as possible. Fighters who telegraph their punches will have them blocked harmlessly by their foes and will leave themselves open to a punishing counterattack.

The unknown causes fear and this can be used to our advantage by keeping our opponent in the dark so far as we are able. Knowledge overcomes fear; therefore the more we can learn of our opponent, the less we will fear. But if we learn that we are overmatched, we can respect our opponent's prowess and avoid the confrontation.

Suppose your car breaks down, and you know that you are not out of gas. Perhaps this exhausts your expertise since you do not know the difference between a carburetor and a distributor. You could locate a fan dancer more quickly than you could find your fan belt. You take the car to a local garage. What do you say to the mechanic? Let's look at several possibilities.

First, "I don't know what's wrong with the car. It suddenly quit. I don't know anything about cars so I can't tell you what the problem is." Second, "When the car stopped, it made a clanking sound so I checked the cam shaft torque and the piston rods. It looks to me like it might be the voltage regulator or the fuel pump." Third, say nothing.

The third approach is much preferable to the other two. In the other two you are making idle conversation. Your primary objective is to get your car fixed, not to win the friendship of the mechanic. Your confession and your speculation contribute nothing to the solution of your problem. They might give you added problems though. Does your diagnosis of the trouble matter to the mechanic, who is trained to find the problem while you are not? The mechanic is paid to do the job, and you will take no part in the repair beyond paying for the work.

The mechanic would only be interested in your confession of ignorance as an opportunity to take advantage of you and increase the charge. He is going to look for the trouble, and fix it if you are fortunate. Whether you get what you pay for and pay for only what you get depends to some extent on how the mechanic sizes you up. When you confess or demonstrate that you are primed for the slaughter, you increase his temptation to skin you. If he is apt to cheat you, make him take a chance and guess your vulnerability; do not make it easy for him. If he decides to cheat you, he may only pad the bill a little.

If the mechanic asks you what's wrong, you can describe any symptoms you are capable of telling accurately. But you should not venture beyond a simple description of what you observed. If he asks further, you can say, "I'm not sure . . . take a look." Let the mechanic find the problem.

For your part, you can ask as many business questions as you like. "Do you give estimates before you begin work?" "How much experience do you have with 1952 Rutabaga sedans?" But when you turn to the repair job itself, you must be careful not to lead with your questions. Base your questions on what he tells you rather than on your speculations. Instead of, "Is it the fuel pump?" ask, "What have you found?"

If he describes symptoms at first rather than explaining the cause, ask, "What does that indicate to you?" As you listen to his explanation knowingly, he may not assume he is speaking to an equal, but he'll probably give you more credit than you deserve.

In order to find out as much as possible about the other side while revealing little of your own, you need to develop several skills including the art of asking questions, the art of listening, and the art of circumvention.

Asking questions keeps the focus of your interchange on your adversary. The information flow is toward you. Asking questions rather than making positive statements softens the interchange and helps to avoid arguments and the tendency to attack or criticize. It checks you from talking too much yourself, but most of all it supplies you with precious information.

As your opponent talks, you get tipped off on his or her strengths and weaknesses, on what he or she wants, and on what he or she is willing to concede. And, getting and keeping your adversary going are not that difficult. Your adversary's interests are your adversary's favorite subjects. The longer you let your opponents expound their wisdom, the smarter they will think you are, and the more they will like you and be willing to bend their positions.

Your first questions should be general, not specific. They should be easy to answer, harmless, and free from controversy. One good way to begin is to ask questions that confirm points you have already agreed on or established or questions that confirm some common ground you share.

Strive for a sincere concern for the other side's point of view. Your manner will show through your questioning, and it will be apparent that you want to maintain a positive personal relationship with your adversary. Show that you are seeking a mutually satisfactory solution which you are confident the two of you can find. Show that you are there to help as you probe your opponent's difficulties sympathetically.

In your probing use open-ended questions that will allow your opponent to speak at length and embellish. In this context avoid questions that call for a yes-or-no response or that can be answered in a simple sentence. Loosen the reins so your adversary can run freely.

The purpose of these questions is to secure information. Therefore, you should eliminate any questions that imply criticism or judgment of the other's position. You are not a prosecutor so pass up the temptation to press your opponent for admissions. This is not the time to use questions offensively. You are not trying to score points at your opponent's expense; you are waiting for your opponent to fumble into your hands. Waiting takes patience.

Do not back your adversary into stating his or her position or demands too early in the session. Once your adversary's position has been stated, he or she will retreat reluctantly and will also preserve the first position as a basis for comparison. Concessions then become more graphic as debate moves farther away from that first position, which your opponent remembers because he or she articulated it. Your questions should gently test and give direction to your opponent's demands so that his or her position is not formulated until the end of your session and is, so far as possible, a product of the session.

Journalists ask questions for a living. If you are stuck for a question, you may be able to borrow from their checklist: who, what, when, where, why, and how. Questions beginning with these words are known to encourage factual responses.

The art of listening completes the job that the art of questioning starts. Unless you listen to your opponent's responses and digest their meaning, your questioning remains an empty exercise in language.

Listening requires that while you hear what is said, you also notice what is not said. Often what is omitted has more significance than what is included. Listening means paying attention to the way your opponent says something as well. Gestures, mannerisms, inflection, and tone convey a message as surely as words. Listening suggests new lines of inquiry and provides a smooth progression to your questioning.

We all have an unfortunate tendency to concentrate on what we are going to say next, causing us to miss much of the other person's message. Even if there is a period of silence while you assimilate the information and decide on your next question, it can only help you. Your adversary may continue speaking in an attempt to explain further.

If you are not clear about what was said, get it straight. Do not decide yourself or guess at the meaning. If you have some doubts, restate the points for confirmation. You can say, "In other words, you mean . . .", or "So, what you're saying is . . ."

Listening takes practice. Perhaps you could try yourself out in ordinary conversations with your friends. When one has finished speaking, see how much of the message you received and from what sources. Perhaps an understanding friend will dissect a conversation with you. In order to be a good listener, you must constantly guard against the tendency to withdraw into your own thoughts. You need to check your focus of attention continually.

Questioning and listening well enable you to find out about

your opponent. The art of circumvention conceals your own position. The object of circumvention is to deflect away inquiries directed at you without seeming evasive. Methods of circumvention available to you include changing the subject, turning the tables, distraction, humor, and exaggeration.

A classic and most effective circumvention is to subtly change the subject. In formal argument this is called shifting the ground. Relevance is a slippery bird not easily caged. By the time your adversary realizes you have changed the subject, if he or she does realize it, you may already be well into the new subject. You may even be able to confuse efforts to return to the original subject by citing relevance yourself. More than likely your opponent's curiosity will blur the idea of relevance enough to allow you to change the subject unobtrusively without a protest.

Turning the tables plays on the principle mentioned earlier that your adversary has a favorite subject—himself (or herself). When asked a question, throw off a one-sentence nonentity and ask the same question yourself. Your adversary will have something to say on the subject or you probably would not have been asked to begin with. If your opinion is asked, you can say, "That's a complicated issue with points on each side. What do you think?" If he or she asks for information say, "It's really hard to be definite," or, "I'd have to look that up. Do you know anything about it?" You dodge and then ask for the same information. If your opponent knows, you can even pay him or her a compliment.

Distraction is a close relative of changing the subject. Instead of shifting to new ground, in distraction you set off on a tangent. Several solid methods of distraction are: telling a story, citing example, and analogizing.

The point under discussion or a pointed question reminds you of a story which you begin to tell. If the story is long enough or good enough, the discussion or question becomes lost in the haze of memory. If the story really does have something to do with the discussion, so much the better. Stories naturally draw our interest and charm us. The urge to know what happens next maintains our attention until we no longer remember or really care about the mundane subject we started with. We may not show it or admit it, but we are still wide-eyed children at bedtime, in the clutch of fantasy and imagination.

Another elusion through distraction involves citing an example. When you are asked a question, you say that the best way to answer the question is through the use of an example. What you don't say is that the use of an example works to your advantage, not to that of the questioner. You launch your example and keep it afloat for a maximum cruise. Once again, it has turned out to be storytime.

Analogy presents another opportunity to dodge a point. There is no such thing as a perfect analogy, and to the extent your analogy is flawed, you have succeeded in distracting your adversary. Two helpful hints on analogy: First, the more you have to explain the facts of the situation being presented in your analogy, the further you can distract your opponent and confuse the discussion.

Second, you will distract your opponent more if you draw him or her into your analogy. For example, your employer asks if you plan to have children. You say, "That question invades my privacy. It is like asking you how much money you put in the collection basket at church on Sunday. Or how often you go to church. Or whether you live up to the tenets of your church." You may distract opponents into thinking about their own stinginess or other failings. You may lead into a discussion on the validity of your analogy. But be sure to know your audience. If it is your boss, you might be fired for your impertinence.

The next tool of circumvention is humor. Have you ever run across people who joke so much you can never really be sure when they are serious and when they are pulling your leg? You are never sure where they stand because no topic is too serious to be joked about. Anything they say may have a double meaning, and they are capable of making almost any statement for the effect it will produce.

Almost every group has someone who is bothered by few limits of taste. If someone else makes a joke about a family member, our joker's mother for instance, he will fabricate in a sharp and serious manner, "That's very funny. My mother died of leukemia earlier this year." His humor can extend to any situation and is ruthless. No one can tell when to take him at face value. He will remain a mystery to his closest friends because his humor conceals his feelings and beliefs. He represents the extreme case of circumvention through humor.

Humor works on the principle of incongruity. We laugh at that which is inconsistent, incompatible, inharmonious, unsuitable—in short, the incongruous. The incongruity of humor defeats the logical progression of ideas and in this way aids circumvention.

Humor also creates a bond between people. It is quite possible to disarm a questioner and at the same time ingratiate yourself with him or her through laughter. The appeal of humor neutralizes a charged atmosphere and mellows feelings, again aiding circumvention. A good sense of humor is probably the most consistent weapon you can have to deflect inquiries and reveal the minimum about yourself.

Two forms of humor deserve special mention: irony and obvious exaggeration. Webster defines irony as the "simulation of ignorance"; also, "a sort of humor, ridicule, or light sarcasm, the intended implication of which is the opposite of the literal sense of the words." These definitions show why irony guards against the revelation of your case. Simulated ignorance and saying the opposite of what you mean for effect will not give your adversary too much help in measuring your case or in figuring you out.

Obvious exaggeration conveys several messages to the questioner. Suppose your spouse or friend asks if you have ever been unfaithful. You answer, "Never more than once a night." Behind the words you are saying to the other person: (1) your question is so obvious that you already know the answer or should know it; (2) I'm so innocent that I can joke about it safely; (3) it's not a serious question and we can treat it lightly; (4) I feel a touch of outrage or hurt that you would suggest such a thing. Best of all, for purposes of circumvention, you have not answered the question. Your obvious exaggeration evades the question while it attacks the concern behind the question which led to it.

You should adopt those forms of circumvention that implement your style. Besides changing the subject, turning the tables, distraction, humor, and exaggeration, there are other approaches to circumvention that fit individual personalities. Aggressive people do not use distraction or humor consistently, as their style generally seeks to intimidate or overwhelm the opponent. They live by the belief that the best defense is a good offense. Remember also that the art of questioning conceals your case by keeping the focus on the other side.

One further point on trying to find out as much about your adversary as possible deserves mention. The principle applies to tactics as well as to the substance of the case. You have to assume that he or she has chosen certain tactics to press the case. You want to find out what they are. Be conscious of the way your opponent is operating. What is your opponent's strategy? Does your adversary try to mislead, ingratiate, or intimidate? Or are some of the devices outlined above being used?

Folklore holds that any general rule worth its keep has an exception. Our rule is to find out as much as possible about your opponent while revealing as little of your own case as you can. The exception to our rule happens when you are confident that your case is strong enough to win. In that event, you may want to open your books and show your opponent what you have so that he or she knows enough to give up or to settle the case. This can save you both the effort of a needless fight.

If you are not sure of your superiority, you should proceed to fight it out. The real danger of deceiving yourself about the merits of your case and about your skillful presentation should warn you against revealing your edge too quickly. This exception only serves your convenience and can be ignored with impunity.

We live in the age of the computer. The information explosion must rank among the most significant developments of our times. On every level—personal, scientific, technical, social, trivial—the body of information is expanding at an increasing rate. Of necessity, the Supreme Court has rewritten the U.S. Constitution to find a right to privacy, unimagined by the drafters, in order to balance the insidious intrusion of the machines of information.

Almost overnight, the right to privacy has reached the forefront among cherished protections because of the pressure of the information explosion. Spying in government and business has never been bigger and must still be regarded as a growing field. The use of informers has become the primary tool in police investigations. Widespread use of immunity by prosecutors in exchange for favorable testimony underlies the criminal justice system.

What does all this tell us about the value of information and the significance of our rule of discovery in a conflict? It might be said that information rivals water as a valuable resource; if water sustains life, then information determines the quality of life.

Every survey of American history contrasts the battle tactics of the British and the colonists. The British, the preeminent military power in the world, marched in ordered columns in the open, wearing stark red coats. When the colonists fired on them, the British showed they were brave by continuing to march in formation while suffering heavy losses.

The colonists, meanwhile, hid behind trees and in the undergrowth. They wore drab everyday clothes that blended in with the forest. They fired and fell back at random to reload and reposition themselves. With these tactics they were able to discuss the day's events with their friends after the battle was over, and they could afford their life insurance premiums.

Think about the British and the colonists. They will help you remember the rule of discovery: find out as much as possible about the other side while revealing as little as possible of your own case.

Chapter 9

Don't Open Your Mouth if You're Not Getting Hurt

Better to remain silent and be thought a fool than to speak out and remove all doubt.
        —*Abraham Lincoln*

One of the hardest lessons to learn is to leave well enough alone. Good lawyers understand this principle because they orient their behavior toward gaining results and forget the rest. They practice economy of speech and effort, an approach that is fairly unusual in the legal profession.

Many lawyers seem incapable of silence no matter how well their case is going for them. One of them, Herb Painstaking, knows the law and works hard. He has his share of intelligence, but sometimes he is just not smart. When he is winning a case, he cannot leave well enough alone and keep his mouth shut. Counselor Painstaking has researched the case; so he must give everyone the benefit of his knowledge. He assumes everyone else must be interested in whatever has caught his interest and in what he has to say about the subject. Herb dissects every minor point in detail to establish his case. He must attack the other side until there is no doubt about their unworthiness.

Winning the judgment is not enough; he must win the popularity contest for his client, too. He boosts his client so that all will admire him and sympathize with his difficulties. By striving to show that his client is faultless on every count and that the opponent must shoulder the blame for the evils of the world, he aims for an overwhelming victory.

Some of this war dance can be explained as Painstaking's effort to earn his fee, but not enough to justify the risk he takes of throwing the case away through some unnecessary error. Because of Herb's flurry of activity, observers might remark, "Painstaking argued a great case but the cards were stacked against him." Agreeing with them, Herb feels good, but he feels good as a loser for his client. He has lost his client's contest because he concentrated on winning a separate contest in which he was the entrant.

Herb is like the outlaw in the formula western. He gets the drop on the guy with the white hat and has all the loot. All he has to do is plug the guy, ride across the Rio Grande, and he's set for life. What does he do? He explains how he pulled off the job, figuring that it does not make any difference because he is going to kill the guy anyway. But if the guy is going to die, what difference does it make if he knows how our desperado got away with the crime? The outlaw is being stupid by trying to convince himself of how clever he is. Not only does he clearly establish his guilt, but he gives the other guy the time he needs to come up with a plan to reverse the positions and get the drop on our talkative bad guy.

A good rule to remember is, if you are not getting hurt, keep your mouth shut. It is just as likely that you will create a problem for yourself as it is that you will solidify your position. Once you have an edge, your strategy should turn conservative, and the bigger your advantage is, the more conservative your style should be. When you gain an edge, the other side must play catch-up. There is no percentage in playing catch-up, so use your favorable odds as a shield.

The law distinguishes between prejudicial error and harmless error. When a case goes up on appeal, the appellate judges look at the record from the trial court. They may find a flock of errors, excesses, and irregularities, but they will not disturb the decision unless they see errors serious enough to prejudice the appealing party by preventing a fundamentally fair hearing.

There is an art in telling the difference between an attack that will materially damage your position and one that will fall harmlessly off your shield. Recognize that there is a difference so that you do not automatically jump to your own defense when challenged. You may breathe life into a dead issue that could come back to haunt you.

Although good lawyers generally know enough to leave well enough alone, some members of the profession have an inconsistent record. Two situations point out this inconsistency while they show in action the principle of leaving well enough alone.

First, during the initial interview with a client, good lawyers are the model of restraint. The client comes in and explains a problem. Do the lawyers say, "With the facts you've given us, you will win your case because the law says such and such"? No, they hedge. They sympathize with the client's problem and say that the client should receive some relief. They will take the case but need some time to verify the best approach under the law as it stands now. The translation of this response reads: it sounds like you have a case worth pursuing, but I have to look up the law to find out because I don't know what the law is.

The laws are stacked so high that it is not difficult to present an experienced general practitioner with a case in an unfamiliar area. Understandably, good lawyers will cover themselves out of a desire for self-preservation. They will research the law later and provide effective representation in the great majority of cases because of their training and mastery of general procedures. But they must guard their image as experts in the law or they will lose their clients' confidence and therefore their clients' business. So they keep quiet.

The second situation occurs at the time for cross-examination of a witness. Here lawyers often fail to show sufficient restraint. The inexperienced lawyer will invariably undertake a cross-examination of the opponent's witness in order to extract an admission that will establish the case. It becomes a God-given right and duty to cross-examine each witness in Perry Mason style to produce the telling admission. The rule of keeping your mouth shut if you are not getting hurt is violated again and again.

Passing up the chance to cross-examine is a hard lesson to learn.

Yet, if you totaled up all the cross-examinations that have been done and averaged out their effectiveness, you would find that the average cross-examination falls short of the effectiveness of not cross-examining. In other words, you get hurt more often than you help yourself.

This is especially true when the testimony of the witness has not damaged your case and doubly true if you do not know what you are after and how you are going to get it when you start your questioning. That witness is not there to help you but is looking for the opportunity to get points across, too. You lose on cross-examination every time you do not win.

Until you spied the pictures on your bookcase, the recent hectic pace of your schedule had not dawned on you. You had asked that new man in your life over for dinner. Lingering over coffee and his compliments for the meal, your conversation explores the polite surface of each other's details. Because he noticed your glance at the bookcase, he comments, "I can see the family resemblance between you and your brother." Silence. He asks a question about your brother. You answer and steer the talk away from the picture. The picture on the bookcase reminded you how busy you were because you had not taken it down. You have a brother, but that's not him. Later on, you will laugh at the irony of your companion's opinion that you resemble his predecessor. If things go well between you, still later you and your new friend may laugh about it together. But for now, you do not open your mouth.

Our rule of leaving well enough alone and keeping your mouth shut if you are not getting hurt has a corollary. Never speak unless you have thought it out. Admissions are common and devastating. Admissions may lose as many cases as all other causes combined. Admissions are statements against interest. In the law, admissions come into evidence in court under an exception to the hearsay rule. In court or outside of court, it is surprising how many times admissions decide the outcome of a conflict.

Because admissions cause so much damage, the only way you can account for the frequency of their appearance is that we just do not think about what we are going to say before we speak. The full significance of our words does not register on us until sometime after they are irretrievably out of our mouth. You have no responsibility to fill up periods of silence with talk. If you find the silence oppressive, bear up and wait a little longer, because before long, someone else will break the silence for you.

The importance of reflection before you speak shows up on cross-examination once again. You must plan your questions in advance. They should be narrow, to the point, and specific. If you ask open-ended questions, witnesses will have the chance to explain or embellish their position, and this narration could easily hurt you. If you ask a general question, witnesses can capitalize on the lack of focus to answer with information different from what you are after. It becomes easier for them to give the answer they want to give instead of the one you are looking for.

You will not be cross-examining witnesses in court, but you will be arguing with people and questioning them on occasions when you run into a problem and find yourself in an adversary position. When this happens, do you want to look good and impress people with your verbal skills while you increase the risk of losing your point through an unnecessary blunder? Or, would you rather keep your own counsel, play the waiting game, and establish your case on your opponent's carelessness? You are presented with precisely this choice often enough for you to follow the rule of keeping quiet if you are not getting hurt. Admissions will continue to rattle around the arenas of argument. Make sure that they are not yours and watch the difference it will make in the results you get.

On the other side of the question, two ways in which you can encourage your adversary to make an admission are to pose the problem inescapably and to use leading questions. Neither technique will work on its own, but either one will nudge people toward concessions which they might be reluctant to make.

Posing the problem inescapably frames the question so that any direct response results in an admission. The well-known, and not very subtle, example of posing the problem inescapably is: "When did you stop beating your wife?" More discreet forms of this technique will return admissions. Rather than answering directly with an admission, the tendency of your adversary when confronted with a question framed in such a way is to explain and justify his actions. The explanation often contains the admissions. Other faults might be confessed in denying the ones mentioned. The answer to the wife-beating question might go something like this: "I might be guilty of a lack of consideration or even a little slap once in a while, but I would never beat my wife."

Leading questions suggest the desired answer as part of the question. "Where were you last night?" is a neutral question. But to give the respondent some hint of the expected answer, you could change the sentence to: "Were you home last night?" The question appears neutral because neither "yes" or "no" is favored, but mentioning the location "home" in the question, instead of waiting for the respondent to supply it, leads to a particular answer.

The classic forms of the leading question are "You were home last night, weren't you?" to suggest a yes answer, and "You weren't home last night, were you?" to suggest a no. If the respondent is cooperating and does not suspect your purpose, you can lead him fairly easily. If you are met with resistance or hostility, you may have success in suggesting the opposite response from the one you desire.

Leading questions and posing the problem inescapably are helpful techniques that may be used to advantage. But, it is far more important for you to remember the basic lessons of this chapter: do not open your mouth if you are not getting hurt. Never speak unless you have thought it out.

To remember the first principle, picture a child in the dentist's chair. The child is paying for too many sweets and not enough brushings. The dentist is poised with the odious drill. Flashing a mouthwash smile, in best chair-side manner, the dentist tolls the victim's death knell: "All right, open up please; this will only take a minute." Our young friend, who is no dummy, has been in this predicament before and has learned from experience: don't open your mouth if you are not getting hurt.

When was the last time you suffered acute embarrassment by committing some social faux pas? Have you ever volunteered for a minor worthy project that seemed to turn into an all-consuming monster, devouring your every spare moment? Do you admit to shortcomings before others inquire? Has someone shown you up badly for espousing a hasty opinion? Remember never to speak unless you have thought it out.

Keep your own counsel and you will not need to look for counsel to get you out of trouble. Silence can have a special kind of eloquence.

Chapter 10

Do Your Homework

The surest road to inspiration is preparation.

—Lloyd George

We now arrive at a topic that admits to no shortcuts, no substitutions, and no bypasses. Preparation is often tedious and unpleasant; it is sometimes dull, but always unavoidable. If it seems burdensome, take consolation in the certainty that preparation is a necessary evil. Doing the groundwork that will prepare you to handle whatever job you face may not be fun, but it is more fun and easier on the stomach than having to perform before you know what you are doing. You will avoid many embarrassing moments and receive handsome returns on the time and effort you spend in getting ready for the job first.

Preparation, the mark of the professional, is known by different names—practice, training, rehearsal, drill, and experience. But the demanding regimen must be followed regardless of the field. Leaving the job to talent alone or to chance will not satisfy the standards of success.

You do not have to be in the class of a fulltime athlete training for the Olympics to gain from preparation. A weekend jogger, for example, needs to plan in advance: a stress test before beginning will confirm the body's capacity for exercise, and a good fit of the proper shoe will prevent strain. Deciding where and when to run is also important—a soft surface will discourage shin splints, and morning or evening coolness will prolong endurance. Warming up with stretching exercises will cut down on muscle pulls. The list could continue on and on. The point is that even something as simple and natural as running can require preliminary work.

The surest road to defeat is complacency. You have the ability to take your fate in your own hands and shape it; so why sit back trusting in the fates and hoping everything will turn out all right? You have the means within your grasp to do the preparation that will change your wishes from a misty dream of "perhaps someday" to the favored odds of "any day now." Even if you are hanging on by your toes, a little legwork will improve your position considerably.

Lawyers have gained a deserved reputation for their attention to detail. The amount of preparation that builds a successful legal argument is substantial. First, the lawyer confers with the client and learns of the complaint or objective. It is necessary to find out what the client is after and what he or she will settle for, even if the client does not know. The lawyer must get to know the client almost as well as the case, recognizing exaggerations and justifications in order to remove them from the operative facts.

A lawyer gathers all the facts and separates the pertinent from the superfluous, researching the area of the law of the case and perhaps conferring with more knowledgeable colleagues. The facts of the case may require other research independent of the law, such as tests of a product's safety and causes of its failure in a mishap. The lawyer must become expert enough in the specialities involved in the case to ask the right questions of the experts and recognize when they overstep the authority of their disciplines.

He or she begins the process of discovery described earlier to learn the strength of the opponent's case and how it can best be attacked. He or she may have to shift through mountains of useless information supplied by the other side, in order to dig out a few nuggets of value.

When all of the information has been collected, the lawyer

organizes it for the most effective presentation. He or she plans the strategy to be used during the fight and modifies it continually as the case progresses to fit changing circumstances. The attorney negotiates with the other side and spars with the other side during the preliminary maneuvers of pretrial motions, conferences, and hearings.

Now if the skirmishing leads to a full-blown fight, the lawyer is prepared for the conflict. He or she has conferred, researched, and gathered information to the point that the fight will almost follow a script. Usually, the battle is not joined but fought out during the preparation stage. If the lawyer neglects preparation of the case, he or she will normally lose.

You do not need to spend three years in law school to enjoy these same benefits of preparation. Give yourself plenty of lead time to prepare for the job. You want to reflect at leisure on the variables that will influence the outcome of the case. Gain a mastery of the facts. Roll them over in your mind until they sink in and you are comfortable with them. Ignore the deceptive comfort of the convenient assumption. Check out your assumptions. Double check and verify your facts.

While preparation is a rational process, the conflict itself and its arguments, which form the end product of the preparation stage, may be highly emotional. Yet emotions have no part to play in the beginning; they distort the results of research and interfere with good preparation.

In preparation you are like a hunter stalking the quarry. You must keep a clear head, plan your assault, and ignore your hunger. The catharsis of emotions must await the kill and the feast.

You need to remain as objective and nonjudgmental as possible during preparation. You should adopt a healthy skepticism toward every approach. Try to attain a dispassionate perspective on your ideas, and develop the faculty of self-criticism. If you can disprove an idea or theory yourself, you will short-circuit your opposition and prevent the damage done by public exposure. Do not fall in love with your theories, the strength of your case, or the power of your brain. The temptation may be great and the justification even greater, but greatest in the end may be the price you have to pay for the luxury of premature celebration.

Good preparation takes persistence, thoroughness, and an exhaustive attention to detail. But once you have run the gauntlet, you are ready for the fight. Serenity will replace doubt. Knowing you have done your best to prepare for the fight will give you added confidence and a positive attitude which will actually improve your performance. And, running the gauntlet is less costly and less painful than being taken by surprise.

What if your adversary catches you off guard? You stand there stunned for several long seconds while you try to regain composure and think of a proper response. However, the pause before you speak can be more eloquent than anything you can come up with: this uncomfortable display will have a powerful effect on your audience.

You are like a prizefighter staggered by a solid punch, but you are not out of the fight. You are still on your feet, although your legs are wobbly and it is obvious that the punch has hurt you. You are in trouble; you must cover up until your head clears, and then you must fight back from behind. And the odds do not smile on those who must play catch-up.

Let us look at an example of the importance of doing your homework. The decision to start a new business provides a case history. While the life expectancy of a new business in the United States exceeds that of a mosquito, it falls short of that of your pet dog or cat. Roughly 80 percent of all new businesses fail within the first three years. They go under before they get established, and the cause of death is the same in the overwhelming majority of cases—poor management. Poor management might mean the business did not have enough capital to sustain its slow beginning; that the inventory was too large or too small; that the appropriate market was not identified or approached in the right way; or that the accounting methods were haphazard. Poor management means that the manager did not do the proper homework.

Before Mary Smith even starts the business, she should already have devoted a great deal of study to the factors that determine if the business will prosper. She spots a need that others have not filled or have not satisfied adequately and identifies those who feel the need. The manager researches to find the best way to make these potential customers aware of a new product or service and the best way to sell them on its value to them. She sets a price that will produce the largest volume while giving the optimum return on effort.

The manager decides what the initial capital outlay should be to sustain the business through its critical infancy. She talks to a banker, hoping to demonstrate that it is a sound investment to loan money on. If she has a retail business, she has to choose a convenient and well-traveled location. She needs to become familiar with the many grinding details that accompany a business: paperwork for the benefit of the business or of the government, dealing with suppliers, a different set of tax forms, regulations, community relations, and so on and on.

When the manager has done the proper homework, she has learned the basic information about general business methods and about her particular type of business. Problems that will arise can then be anticipated, and the manager will be ready to handle them when they appear. An estimated tax payment will not come by surprise and dangerously deplete working capital. Nor will a flurry of business create shortages that could lead to dissatisfied customers who will take their business elsewhere.

If the business goes belly up, the manager can afford to be philosophical. She gave it the best shot possible. The manager, being human, may have made a mistake in judgment; no vaccine will inoculate against human error. But she has no regrets about the attempt when everything was prepared as well as possible. Second thoughts and recriminations grow out of the failure to prepare, not the failure to accomplish. And the one who prepares will fail less often.

Attempts to persuade an audience also require preparation. You may get by on your charm and facile tongue, but why leave it to chance? There are a number of steps that go into preparing a persuasive appeal. Imagine that you are starting a business and plan to ask your banker for a loan. Apply the following steps to help prepare for the meeting with the banker.

1. Begin with the general preparation of research, fact gathering, and analysis. What facts are important? Which ones will impress the audience? Where do the facts lead to a contrary conclusion and how can you minimize this?

2. Study the audience and the situation. Whom are you seeking to persuade? What is the occasion? What attitudes does the audience hold, and what are the underlying personal and social reasons for those attitudes? What is likely to influence the audience?

3. Organize the material. Prepare an outline of the arguments you will use and the evidence, tailored to the audience and occasion, that supports your arguments.

4. Practice your presentation until you are comfortable with it. Revise the material until it flows smoothly. Concentrate on the weak links and the parts you have trouble with.

5. Make notes of key words or phrases that will jog your memory on the main points you want to make. Memorize the key words if you do not plan to have notes with you.

6. Visualize the scene and play it out in your mind as it is likely to occur. Shortly before the meeting, verbalize your presentation so the polished delivery will remain fresh in your mind.

You can apply these six steps with your own modifications to a variety of persuasive situations such as interviews, conversations, speeches, telephone calls, or meetings. With the storehouse of material that an organized preparation will generate, you will feel competent to handle objections or resistance. You will assert your position more effectively because you will have the confidence of support for your arguments. You will expect a favorable result. And, that should be a reasonable expectation.

We admire the skill of a great courtroom lawyer such as F. Lee Bailey. When we see the finished product, we forget the work that went into the performance. Because of his ability and position, Bailey is the focus of our attention among a team of his people who are preparing the case. He draws on a staff of lawyers and investigators who do the background work.

As he argues the case, he does not enumerate all of the preliminary steps that have contributed to his presentation. He immerses himself in a case, laboring long hours to absorb as much information as possible before the fight begins. Preparation is more obvious in its absence; it can be overlooked when it has been done well, but will usually be noticed when it has not been done.

If you know that you have done your homework, you will have the peace of mind and acceptance of the future that go with having done your best to get ready. The bonus will come in the form of better results.

Chapter 11

Anticipate the Other Side

The ability to raise searching difficulties on both sides of a subject will make us detect more easily the truth and error about the several points that arise.

—Aristotle

Our vast country offers a variety of climates and living conditions. From the deserts of Arizona and New Mexico to the rain forest of Washington and Oregon, from the marshy glades of Florida and Georgia to the plains of Nebraska and the Dakotas, each region exhibits a strong local character. And each of these areas has its die-hard adherents. One person's wasteland is another person's paradise.

No one doubts the loyalist's belief that he or she has found paradise in the peculiar beauty of a certain region. But if we gathered one booster from each region together in a room, would even one of them be convinced by another's argument? Probably not. Yet each one would probably be quite sure of winning many of the others over to the beauty that he or she finds so obvious.

Similarly, when you take a position, the position can sometimes take possession of you as well. Like the sea to a sailor or the earth to a farmer, it can become a part of you.

It is easy to let down your guard and allow your argument

to seduce you into a state of overconfidence. You forget that your argument has one or more rivals for the beauty title. You overlook the imperfections that appear insignificant in judging the whole. You may hide even larger faults under your expert makeup job. You cannot qualify as an impartial observer of your argument's attributes; you cannot assess the worth of your case in the vacuum of a one-sided preparation.

One-sided preparation produces a slanted viewpoint and an inflated opinion of the strength of your argument. This problem can create a weakness in your case that leaves it vulnerable to attack. Because you do not see the flaws in your argument clearly, you will not be ready to shore them up or to sidestep your opponent's attack. The solution to this problem is to prepare both sides of the case.

Anticipating the other side is the essential game in international relations. Each nation must preoccupy itself with the rumblings of its competitors and neighbors. To protect national security, the tacticians of defense, casting suspicious eyes in all directions, examine the intelligence collected by their own forces and the proclamations and movements issuing from the other side for indications of what others intend to do. The cold war may have thawed in the last twenty-five years, but the human race does not yet recognize its brotherhood, and anticipating the other side remains the lifeblood of a nation's survival.

On an individual level when you start by arguing for the opposite result from the one you desire, you gain a perspective on your position. You can appreciate the merits of the other point of view. If you can more easily discover where each side is strong and weak, you will know where you should concentrate your efforts.

By anticipating how your opponent will approach the case, you can be ready for his or her probable moves. In other words, if you know which aspects of your opponent's case are most vulnerable, you can decide more effectively how your attack should take advantage of this vulnerability.

You should be able to recognize the weak links in your own argument and be able to minimize their damage. Before the action begins, make sure you have time to plan how you will manage your soft spots. For example, you might steal your adversary's thunder by pointing out your own weaknesses in a sympathetic light or you may unearth an argument that shifts the ground away from them. At the least your opponent will not surprise you by raising objections you were not aware of and perhaps cause you to panic or become flustered.

In anticipating the other side, you must estimate your opponent's strength and judge where it resides. You must predict the other side's attack so you will not be caught off guard. A good way to do this is to take that case and prepare it yourself; this will give you firsthand experience of the other viewpoint.

For example, you hurt your back at work when you tilted your chair back too far under the influence of a potent daydream. You need income to weather your recuperation so you apply for workmen's compensation.

You have done your homework and found that you must establish that your injury was work related in order to qualify for benefits. When you place yourself in the examiner's position, your reasoning goes as follows: this guy is not a circus performer. Balance acts aren't part of the job. Therefore a chair used properly represents no danger. The risk was created outside of the scope of normal activities, and the victim should bear the responsibility for being careless. You notice that the examiners will probably focus on the tilting of the chair itself and its risk, so your presentation must respond to this inclination.

Your plan is to tie your action to a job-induced reverie. You portray the scene from the beginning with emphasis on the heavy concentration your job demands. You shift the responsibility for the tilting, away from your preference for comfort and toward the mental absorption your job requires, which would blot out anyone's awareness of the physical surroundings. The stresses of your job caused your tilting of the chair unconsciously. The emphasis on the job's role in your downfall should cause the examiner to lean in your direction.

Debaters exemplify the value of getting the balanced perspective that comes from arguing both sides of a question. Each year there is one issue assigned for debate. During the course of the year, most teams will advocate each side of the issue many times. Any one team may excel at the affirmative or negative because of chemistry, conviction, or personality, but each team improves at arguing either side as it gains experience in debating the opposite conclusion.

The law concerns itself for the most part with rights in conflict. The development of the law follows the resolution of those conflicts. Judges earn their keep by making the difficult decisions that choose between rights when they clash. Usually, there are two sides to a case that reaches court. If there were not merit in each position, the case would already have been settled.

If the parties knew which one of them had a superior position, they would not need to fight it out in order to prove who is deserving. One could graciously concede the victory to the other and save the headaches. But the outcome of most cases defies accurate prediction. There is no clear-cut division between the good guys and the bad guys. Legal issues will not break down into a comfortable pattern or a black-and-white choice.

In the law, there are two ways to posit a case: you can speak of the rights of the plaintiff or of the duties of the defendant. A shift in emphasis from one perspective to the other will change the character of the case. When you want to anticipate the other side by arguing its position, you should keep this added dimension in mind. Translated into common terms, the rights of the plaintiff denote what you are entitled to get, and the duties of the defendant specify what must be given.

Suppose you face a situation in which you want to fight for something you are entitled to get. To prepare for the conflict you should also consider the issue from the perspective of what your opponent must give, as it may be different. You should also consider both perspectives from your opponent's viewpoint. Four different slants ought to get you off to a good start:
1. Plaintiff's view of what he or she is entitled to get
2. Plaintiff's view of what defendant is obliged to give
3. Defendant's view of what plaintiff is entitled to get
4. Defendant's view of what he or she is obliged to give

Lawyers must toil in this uncertain field with dual perspectives and shades of gray. Possibly their disputacious natures prefer the stimulation of the competition, and they would languish in a more predictable arena. If conflict sustains them, they should thrive, because their diet includes a goodly portion of close cases and nuances of meaning. Yet their goal is still to make the fight as uneven in their favor as they can.

Enter the tool of discovery. Lawyers try to find out as much as possible about the opposing case and at the same time to put their own case in order. Studying what the other side has and what an adversary might do constitutes a large part of the job of getting one's own case in shape. The process follows almost a dialectic form. With the information supplied by the tools of discovery, lawyers can piece together the other side's arguments. Anticipating the strategy of the other side is necessary so that a good response will be ready. Perhaps the most effective technique for anticipating the actions of your opponents is to step into their shoes, take on their assignments, and argue those positions at the beginning.

Science operates in a similar manner. The scientific method has accelerated the advancement of knowledge and led to innumerable discoveries that have improved the quality of our lives. But it does not search out the answers to problems. The scientific method works in the opposite direction from what many people believe. It has a negative rather than a positive character in that it posits a possible solution and then tries to discredit it.

Scientists do not conduct experiments that seek to establish a scientific principle or that something is true. They formulate a hypothesis and then try to disprove it. They make an educated guess and then attack its validity. Their hypothesis stands until someone else comes along with a better one.

The value of the discipline is the scientists' attitude toward their ideas. While they may respect their ideas, able scientists will never fall in love with them but will test them ceaselessly. Ideas must constantly earn respect. Scientists must challenge their strength without pause and keep them under observation. Upon finding a flaw, the scientist mercilessly discards the hypothesis and looks for another one. With this rigorous process, any ideas that survive deserve their place in the sun.

If we required a like degree of justification for our arguments, they would serve us well. Experiment with the negative attitude of the scientist. Adopt a healthy skepticism toward your case, and see if you can shoot it down. If you take an adversary stance against your case by arguing the other side, you will be prepared for whatever your opponent throws at you.

If your objective is persuasion, the catchword is empathy. In persuasion you anticipate the feelings and the desires of the other instead of the arguments. Empathy means the imaginative projection of your consciousness into another being. You feel as he or she would feel, and you react to the situation the same way he or she would. You see the subject from the other's frame of reference.

To persuade another person to your point of view, you must project yourself into his or her state of mind and recognize what approach will complement that way of thinking. You will find the other person to be more receptive to your ideas and directions when you anticipate how he or she will respond to various overtures, and you select the approach that most closely fits those attitudes, beliefs, and values. After you identify the other person's goals, you then identify your message with those goals. The listeners' prejudices and perceptions have more influence on his or her acceptance of your message than the strength of your facts or the power of your delivery style.

One method to encourage your empathizing with the other person is to explore the common ground between both sides. Discover the interests, opinions, and ambitions that you have in common, then dwell on your areas of agreement and slide over your differences. When you emphasize the thoughts and feelings you share with another person, you engender a feeling of closeness.

When the other person feels a bond between the two sides, there is more of a tendency to accept suggestions you might put forward. With this sense of belonging grows a willingness to go along with the ideas you volunteer. If you seem to be speaking the same language, the other party will be susceptible to suggestions, and it is possible to persuade him or her that your ideas express opinions that he or she already holds. Anticipate the other side's feelings, share them and express your message in those common terms.

What do competitive sports, the military, and big business have in common? Scouting reports. The lesson of this chapter is to anticipate the other side by arguing the case from the other viewpoint during your preparation. To help you remember the message of this chapter, remember the words *scouting report*. The scouting report is the product of studying the adversary's strengths and weaknesses. You use a scouting report to construct your own case and to plan strategy. Prepare a scouting report on your opponent's arguments; you will know what to expect during the battle, and you will be ready to handle it.

Chapter 12

Get the Facts

Knowledge is of two kinds. We know a subject ourselves, or we know where we can find information upon it.

—Samuel Johnson

Mr. and Mrs. Lurche were enjoying a quiet Sunday afternoon reading the paper when Mr. Lurche spotted a classified ad which he excitedly showed his wife. It read:

Vacation Retreats
Mountain acreage for as little as $195 an acre
Waterfront, Good financing
Write Uncle Eddie, P.O. Box ZZ
Slippery Snake, Washington

The Lurches had been dreaming of the day when they could afford their own hideaway. Now they had found one within their means. They wrote away to Eddie that day for the details.

A week later, the eagerly awaited information packet arrived. They pored over glossy color brochures showing smiling families fishing, water-skiing, barbecuing, swimming, and hiking. Rustic cabins, perfect for roughing it comfortably, nestled among the birches and the pines and had beautiful views of the sandy beach along the lake. Everything they saw fulfilled their expectations. The pace of their excitement quickened.

Mr. Lurche looked over the terms of the contract enclosed with the material. The financing was confusing, with payments of different amounts due at different times. It seemed as if Uncle Eddie was neither sophisticated nor used to dealing with complicated computations. The interest rate seemed high and the prices were higher than $195.00, but they were still far below the market.

The Lurches agreed they would be throwing money away to pass up a bargain like this. Was it any concern of theirs if Uncle Eddie was some old trapper who had stayed in the woods too long and was not getting full value for his land? When Mrs. Lurche expressed a lingering doubt about whether it might not be too good to be true, Mr. Lurche calmed her with an explanation about how this move would be an excellent investment for them, returning their money several times over in a few years and still providing a recreation site for them for as long as they owned it.

Only a limited number of properties were available, and they had to act soon to avoid a scheduled price increase. So they selected a lakefront lot, filled out the contract, and wrote out a check. They spent the next several days in the glow of satisfaction caused by their timely decision and looked forward to their summer vacation.

We next visit the Lurches at the end of summer as they confer with their attorney. Surprisingly, or maybe not so surprisingly, they want to sue Uncle Eddie to get out of their contract. When they arrived at their little paradise, they found pine trees and birch trees, but little else except a mass of tangled underbrush.

They did not expect to find a cabin on their property; they had a camper. But there were no other cabins around either—not so much as an outhouse. That there was no beach was bad enough but even worse was the apparition that Uncle Eddie had termed a lake. Calling it a marsh might even be stretching the truth a bit. The water was deep enough for mosquitos to swim in, but a good-sized frog would have to pick spots to practice his kicking.

Disturbed as they were by all they saw when they arrived, the Lurches were even more outraged by the way they had arrived. They had chartered a helicopter. The closest access for their camper was a dirt road that ended fifteen miles short of their property. The helicopter pilot had cleared a place to land the two or three customers each summer who were curious enough to see their paradise after making the long trip north.

The Lurches had discovered enough bad news themselves. Now their lawyer took a turn and told them Uncle Eddie had assigned his rights under the contract to Fast Fast Freddie's Finance Co. Freddie appeared to be what the law calls a holder in due course; this means he would take the contract free of the defenses the Lurches might have against Eddie. If this were the case, the Lurches could not sue Freddie for Eddie's misbehavior.

To compound the fracture, the practicality of a suit against Eddie was not impressive. Just tracking him down in the woods to serve him with a complaint would be tough. But perhaps they should try to sue Eddie anyway because of the amount of money involved. The lawyer then outlined the "unsophisticated" balloon payments and escalator clauses in Eddie's contract which pushed the Lurches' obligation to several times the size they had expected.

Regrettably, time and a squeamish sense of compassion dictate that we must leave the Lurches out on their shaky limb at this point of the story. They have served our purpose of stressing the need to get the facts. Get the facts first; get all the facts; get the facts straight.

In the Lurches' case, a visit with their attorney before making the offer would have educated them about the facts of the financing. At a minimum, an on-site inspection of the property should precede any offer to buy. Asking for the names of other customers, checking with government and business organizations such as the Federal Trade Commission and the Better Business Bureau about Eddie's reputation, and talking with local people who are familiar with Eddie's operation would also have been wise.

Experienced lawyers have developed conditioned reflexes to the gathering of facts. Their automatic response to clients at the beginning of the case is to find out as precisely as possible what happened. Perhaps they will have a client narrate the chain of events from beginning to end, or maybe they will test a client's recall about some occurrences and ask for further explanation of others. They may probe to some extent to verify that a client has made a sincere effort to relate knowledge fairly and evenly.

Some people have especially selective memories, and others,

who are natural storytellers, cannot help exaggerating facts and improving on reality. A few will outright lie if they can get something out of it. The client's version begins a process of investigation and research for the lawyer that we touched on earlier, but the facts still form the starting point.

The facts constitute more than the foundation of the case. Certainly a case rests on a shaky foundation when you do not have a firm grasp on the facts or when the facts favor your opponent. But the facts also encompass the majority of the total building materials that make up the finished product. Shoddy construction caused by not getting the facts first, not getting all the facts, or not getting the facts straight will bring your case tumbling down around you.

Even before the word *credibility* was introduced into our everyday vocabulary by the Watergate unravelings, it had attained a high place in the language of the law. There is nothing so precious to the lawyer arguing in court as credibility in the presentation of the case. Few things will evaporate credibility faster than being caught misstating the facts. It is downright embarrassing to have the assumed facts underlying your argument stripped away, leaving you standing naked and looking for the illusory, gracious way to say, "Never mind." It is quite certain that factual error can fatally wound a winning case.

The reason for the great importance that the facts play in a case's outcome lies in the primary emphasis the law places on the facts. Contrary to popular belief, and the belief of many lawyers, the power of precedents (rules of law from prior cases that guide the judge on how the present, similar case should be resolved) does not equal the power of the facts to determine the result of a case. Ultimately, the rule of law holds sway at the pleasure of what is reasonable under the facts of the particular case. The ubiquitous *reasonable,* the most powerful word in the law, in effect says to look to the facts of the case.

If we have sufficiently emphasized the importance of the facts, now is the time to pause for a moment to consider exactly what a fact is. How would you define a fact? It is difficult to pin down a good working definition without becoming a semanticist or a philosopher. Perhaps, like obscenity, we will know a fact when we see it even though precise definition escapes us.*

The dictionary tells us that a fact is "that which has actual existence"; "the quality of being actual"; "the statement of a thing done or existing." That helps somewhat; yet, those phrases still seem vague and not especially descriptive. In a nutshell, maybe the best working definition of a fact is a true statement or an actual event.

We should be concerned with defining the word precisely to enhance our understanding, but the brunt of our efforts relates to the uses to which we put the facts. Defining the facts assumes less importance than identifying, tracing, building on, and manipulating them as we shape an argument. From this viewpoint we look upon facts as the stuff of our argument—the ingredients of our persuasion.

The job gets sticky when we try to separate the facts from the chaff. We hardly ever remember events in exactly the way they happened. It is difficult to see, hear, and feel with accuracy; our senses are easily duped. We begin interpreting at the same time that we are experiencing the event. In addition, because of subjective differences, each person will see an event in a different light.

Our brains take an active role in deciding what our senses will pick up, and decide solely how the stimuli will be interpreted. Just as a settled married couple might finish each other's sentences, we interact with what we experience to round the corners and polish the surface. As an event recedes in our memory, our mind will work on it until we remember what should have been as much as what actually was. While our consciousness remains innocently idle, our subconscious works on our memories until they achieve a comfortable fit with our attitudes, expectations, and values.

Maybe knowing a fact when we see it is not as easy as it seems: opinions, conclusions, suspicions, desires, gossip, abstractions, assertions, and generalities often masquerade as facts. Calling a

---

*The Supreme Court has grappled unsuccessfully for a definition of obscenity for decades. One justice in a famous opinion said in effect that he could not define obscenity but he knew it when he saw it.

thing a fact can cover a lot of loose thinking, but saying it does not make it so. We must distinguish true statements and actual events from deceptively packaged imitations.

The law draws a distinction between facts and conclusions. A witness should testify to the facts, but not to conclusions. It is up to the judge or jury to draw conclusions from the facts presented. After the witnesses tell what they saw and heard and relate the raw material gathered by their senses, the judge has to sort through this material to find its significance. Preparing an argument by collecting its underlying facts is like preparing a witness for testifying. You should travel back from conclusions to the facts that form the basis for those conclusions.

Because lawyers seek causes, they treat every piece of evidence as an effect and pursue the root causes until they are satisfied that they have reached the source. They treat every statement as a conclusion and track its supporting facts. This is a good safeguard. Then they can relax with the assurance that they have a mastery of their materials—a solid grip on the facts. Until someone shows you otherwise, assume any statement is a conclusion that hides a series of antecedent facts.

Let us construct an example of the journey from conclusion back to the facts. Suppose you want to convince your friend Mike that he should quit his job. The conclusion of your argument— that he should quit his job—is also a fact because it is a true statement to you. But it may only be your opinion or assertion and not a true statement. You have not verified its validity merely by stating it, especially for your friend who might disagree with you.

To organize the evidence for your argument, you need to travel back from your conclusion to show its factual basis. To travel back from your conclusion, you ask Why? or What is the basis? at each level you reach.

Thus: Mike should quit his job. Why? He is not suited for that type of work, and it is apparent that his talents lie elsewhere. His chances for promotion are poor. Why? He is unhappy and unproductive. He is not himself. Why? He has been depressed and tense. He has missed a lot of work. He has been irritable and doesn't get along well with his coworkers. He has gotten drunk frequently. What is your basis for saying he was drunk? You saw him drink a great deal of alcohol on too many occasions. His speech was slurred, movements were slow and unsteady, and in fact he staggered.

What is the basis for saying he staggered? His steps were of unequal lentghs, their timing was irregular, and his direction changed. He reached for furniture and the wall to support himself and almost fell although his path was clear. What is the basis for saying his direction changed? Now we have reached the empirical level of measurement. We answer in directions, feet and inches, and angles and degrees in describing the dimensions of the room and deviations from the starting point.

We have followed a certain course in our tracking. But each conclusion at any one level has any number of supporting facts at the previous level. We could have listed the string of facts leading us to conclude that he was drinking a great deal of alcohol (label on bottle, smell of liquid, amount when he started compared to amount left after he drank, etc.) rather than following the trail of his staggering.

This is the reasoning process you should adopt to separate what lawyers call the ultimate facts from derivative facts. By analyzing your subject in this manner, you will cut through the layers of abstraction and generality that you naturally build on observable facts. You will have a better idea of whether your conclusions are valid and if you can support your contentions in an argument with an evidentiary basis of fact.

The lower your level of abstraction and the more particular your facts, the stronger and more vivid your argument will be. Solidify your argument by traveling back through the layers of conclusions to the particular facts. But most important, get the facts first; get all the facts; and get the facts straight.

All are not created equal in the realm of fact. Facts are endowed by their creators with certain exaggerations and distortions, and they have different degrees of reliability. When someone supposedly relates facts to you, you want to be able to recognize whether you can trust that person's accuracy. We are now looking at the other side of the question. Which of the assertions presented to you as fact can you rely on?

The factors that influence the reliability of facts include interest, capacity, affinity, motive, age, corroboration, credentials, consistency, and manner. Let us find out what each of these means in more detail.

Interest refers to the stake, if any, that the narrator has in what he or she tells. We can more readily accept what disinterested witnesses might say because they have nothing to gain or lose by manipulating the facts to influence our opinions. For example, we might be wary of what an oil executive says about the supply of energy.

Capacity is the ability of the narrator to observe accurately, to understand what he or she has seen, and to relate it accurately. The quality of the narrator's memory is a part of this capacity. Obviously, the longer the time period between the occurrence of the event and the narration by the witness, the greater the importance memory assumes. Capacity becomes an issue when the witness is a child, suffers from mental or emotional problems, observed the event under some stress, or was under the influence of alcohol or drugs. An English citizen has greater capacity than a French-Canadian to describe what happened at a cricket match but should defer if the game is ice hockey.

Affinity stands for the relationship between the narrator and the facts. We distinguish firsthand knowledge from secondhand, thirdhand, and so on. The concern with the connection between the narrator and the facts supplies the rationale for the exclusion of hearsay testimony in court. Witnesses who have observed something firsthand are more reliable than witnesses who have learned their information from someone else who observed the event. The latter is more reliable than a witness who has learned the information from someone who read an account in the newspaper. Each additional step from the firsthand knowledge of direct observation or experience adds another opportunity for error.

Motive is the reason the witness tells the story. What is the stimulus that prompted him or her to become involved in an event, and what induces his or her statement? Can you isolate a personal incentive such as monetary gain or satisfaction of some desire?

Age refers to the age of the facts. A fact can be fresh or stale just like a clue, a trail, or a doughnut. With the expansion of knowledge, information becomes obsolete. Old evidence is less reliable and should be kept up to date by discarding information as it loses its currency. What was significant yesterday becomes today's museum piece or curiosity. The future assaults the present and turns working facts into idle trivialities. While memories haze over, facts die and can be reborn in unrecognizable shapes.

Corroboration concerns the amount of accompanying evidence that supports the witness. If some number of other people tell the same story, we have a greater basis for accepting the truth of a witness's statements. Corroboration includes the other forms of evidence that back up a fact. Our own experience can corroborate what another tells us, and, in fact, the presence of corroboration is much more important than the degree of corroboration. In other words getting a second witness is crucial; getting a third, fourth, or fortieth is gravy, more or less.

Credentials involve the status of the narrator. What is his or her level of training, expertise, experience, or reputation? Reputation especially includes the reputation for truth and honest conduct. How do these qualities relate to the facts at hand? An eminent theologian may possess greater training and expertise than the pope, but few Roman Catholics would choose another's theological opinion over that of the pope, in light of the pope's reputation. The experience of the Wright brothers outweighed the expertise of contemporary engineers on the question of flight by a heavier-than-air craft. You must balance the value of these qualities in each case to see which ones will fly.

Consistency covers both the relationship between the facts themselves and the relationship between the facts that the witness relates and external facts. Any contradictions or inconsistencies naturally cast suspicion on the narration and reduce its reliability.

Finally, the reliability of what is alleged as fact can be tested by the manner of narration. Attuning yourself to body language provides meaningful nonverbal messages. Poor eye contact, shifting positions, nervous gestures, sweating, and halting speech are among the manifestations of deception that betray a witness. Such behavior does not establish that a witness is lying, but it does raise the possibility. These are only indications. For some people, these mannerisms are a permanent part of their makeup. Take care to reserve judgment until you have eliminated the possibility that the witness is sincere and only showing nervousness.

Whether you are preparing your own arguments or whether you must assess another's case that is being presented to you, your job is the same. Travel back from conclusions to the facts. Get the facts first, get all the facts, and get the facts straight.

In his book *The Lawyers,* Martin Mayer cites a survey of Harvard Law graduates:

> A 1947 sample survey of Harvard Law School alumni asked respondents to rank in order of importance six lawyerly skills: "negotiation, draftsmanship, advocacy, legal planning, 'knowing the law' in a practical sense (the ability to predict how cases will be decided), and ability to secure an understanding of facts and motives." The numerical rankings were then averaged for each skill, and five of them were pretty well bunched; the solitary leader, by a big margin, was the ability to deal with facts and motives.*

As those of our profession like to say, I rest my case.

---

*New York: Dell, 1968, p. 97. Reprinted by arrangement with Harper & Row.

Chapter 13

Think Different Ways

One must learn to think well before learning to think; afterwards it proves too difficult.

—Anatole France

Our brains remain active whether we are waking or sleeping. Well, let's give ourselves the benefit of the doubt. With all that activity, you would expect impressive results. Sometimes we can really surprise ourselves with our ideas and insights. Yet at other times we get bogged down and are easily frustrated.

When we encounter a problem, we think about it and turn it over and over in our mind. The solution eludes us. The problem dominates our thoughts and torments us, and we find ourselves in a rut, going over the same dead ends again and again.

Maybe we start talking to ourselves, urging ourselves to continue the fight and offering words of encouragement. Often it seems that the harder we press, the farther we seem to get from the solution. Once we become distracted, we start thinking about our thinking and the difficulties we are having, and the possibility of solving the problem becomes even more remote.

Some of this suffering is inevitable in our imperfect world. But we can reduce our difficulties and improve our results if we organize our thought processes to take advantage of our strengths.

If we substitute a conscious effort to harness our mental energy for a haphazard assault on a problem, we will enhance the quality of our thinking itself and of its end product.

Computers perform amazing feats. Their functions have steadily increased. Compared with people, they are faster, more thorough, and more disciplined. People make mistakes, but computers are unerring.

Despite their advantages, computers cannot yet match our brain-power. They still rely on programmers and the precision of the program. Compared to the computer, people are versatile, imaginative, flexible, independent, and brilliant. And most important, what separates people from computers is our ability to experience, to remember what we experience, and to find meaning in it.

Yet these attributes that provide our very strength can be our own worst enemy. They can send us down the wrong track, encourage us to continue down a dead end path, or distract us from a thorough, even pursuit of a solution. If we can emulate the cold-blooded computer in its systematic search and channel our strengths into a more organized pattern, our thinking will bear more fruit.

Thinking, in a phrase, is the manipulation of memory. When you face a problem, you look to past experiences for guidance. A similar situation may offer an analogy. A pattern from the solution of another problem may be overlaid on the present problem. You want to jog your memory into supplying a stream of potential solutions, patterns, and approaches from past successes. With enough sparks from our experience our memory will ignite the materials of our problem. In the glow of the flames, the outline of the solution will appear.

Strictly speaking, original thought does not exist. Thoughts are built on the ideas and discoveries of the past; originality only enters when new arrangements, new combinations, or new perspectives create a distinct product out of familiar ingredients.

Our goal in thinking through a problem is the exhaustive manipulation of our memory. We want to vary our approach, and therefore we attack the problem on as many fronts as our imagination can establish. By purposefully calling into play the breadth of our experience, we learn to think in different ways.

There is nothing we can do to increase our innate mental ability. We are stuck with the mind we have, but we can broaden our experience. It is a slow, imperceptible process that rewards us far beyond the benefits it provides to our thinking. But the growth is gradual and depends on our will to persevere in a life-style that chases experience and fosters knowledge. However, we will notice a more immediate improvement in our thinking from a conscious attempt to organize our efforts and to pursue the solutions to problems systematically.

A man named Graham Wallas did pioneer work in the field of thinking by identifying four steps in problem solving—preparation, incubation, illumination, and verification. These steps provide a bare outline for the progression of the thinking process. You may find them helpful as a quick checklist on your attempt to solve a problem.

Preparation, of course, means that you must do your homework. You need to learn as much about the problem and its background information as you can absorb in the time allowed. You should adopt a questioning attitude and only reluctantly accept even basic assumptions at face value. Every detail should be observed and every relationship noted. Try to find associations among your facts and between your facts and the facts of other situations and other solutions.

You should project possible outcomes, using different arrangements of the facts. Try to predict a number of potential solutions to the problem. If the solution surfaces during these efforts, be grateful for your luck and relax until the next problem. In the usual case of a challenging problem, preparation leads to incubation.

Once you have absorbed the information, back off, put the problem to one side, and let the recesses of your mind play with the data. Do not force things. Your mind works better untrammeled, and it takes time for the solution to take root and take form.

The incubation period could last several seconds or several months. The length of time depends on the problem, on your state of mind, on your preparation, and on many other factors. The incubation stage is finished when the contours of a solution begin to take shape. If the solution stubbornly remains absent for what you consider an excessive length of time, review and perhaps add to your preparation.

Illumination can come with the suddenness of "Eureka! I've found it!" and supply an obvious solution. More often, the last step of verification is necessary. You measure the solution in terms of the problem to verify its validity. If you find the solution wanting, you return to your preparation.

During the preparation step, which is the only stage in which you do any real work, there are three basic approaches to solving a problem—brainstorming, classification, and cause and effect.

Alex Osborn, an advertising executive, popularized the idea of brainstorming, in his book *Your Creative Power*. He supplied a large list of questions that characterize the brainstorming method, including the following: To what other uses can this be put? Is there something similar I could partially copy? What if this were somewhat changed? What can I substitute? How else can this be arranged? What if this were reversed? What could I combine this with?

In brainstorming you let your mind roam free and open yourself to any ideas no matter how useless they might seem. It is important to suspend your critical powers during this process, and dispel any inhibitions that will curtail the free flow of ideas. Free association is the order of the day. Think different ways—logically, literally, imaginatively, recklessly, whimsically, universally, specifically, fantastically. When you brainstorm it, you dream the impossible dream. Who knows, even if you do not solve the problem, you might become a famous poet.

You must develop the ability to spot things that are hard to distinguish from their background. Your goal is to look at the problem in a new light that will illuminate the solution. You are not exploring the problem so much as you are searching your own mind. You seek from your memories a pattern, which is usually not applied to this type of problem, that fits it. You must detach your thoughts from habitual tracks and range over a wide assortment of possible patterns, welcoming mental frameworks far removed from the ordinary and the established.

You are trying to find some factor that can be moved or changed and should pay attention to all ideas—even if they seem irrelevant and unsuitable. They may have popped up for a reason, and they may become the key factor in locating the solution. As the word indicates, brainstorming is a volatile mechanism.

The second approach, classification, contrasts with brainstorming in that it is orderly, structured, and deliberate. In classification you try to solve a problem by finding which familiar categories the information might fit. You line up the unsettled and the unknown against the settled and known to learn which groups can assimilate the unknown and reveal some of its secrets. The philosopher John Dewey identified a classification as a repertory of weapons for attack upon the future and the unknown.

If you want to identify the features of the problem that coincide with features of accepted methods or proven ideas, exhaustive listing has enormous value. You label and sort until the information almost forms the appropriate pattern itself. Like a good filing system, the hard work in classification comes in setting it up, and its usefulness hinges on the validity and precision of the labels and the categories.

Let us run through an example to see the classification approach in action. The problem you must solve is to find a new doctor, and you are already well under way because you have identified the problem. This is a major step because sometimes you do not know what the problem is, and the bulk of your job is to discover the problem. When you expend a lot of effort in identifying the problem, often the solution is close behind.

Review the methods used previously to find a lawyer, other doctors, different kinds of brokers, a daycare center, insurance agent, a rare or unusual product, or even a vacation spot. How have other people approached the problem? Ask friends and acquaintances how they would go about it. What skills and personality traits are important? What variables such as location, recommendations, availability, waiting time, cost, treatment philosophy, support personnel, and hospital affiliation count heavily? What other variables can you think of?

What substitutes are available, such as relying on emergency room care, joining a group medical plan, or finding a community or university clinic? What are the alternatives to seeking out a doctor? What if you do nothing? What is the role of preventive medicine or home remedies? What is the nature of your job? What other jobs have similar obstacles and how are they handled? You should continue to strain the brain along these lines until you are inundated with a list of similar situations and similar patterns.

The third approach in preparation is the cause-and-effect method. Facts and ideas do not exist in a void. Events do not occur randomly. The cause-and-effect method structures your thinking to take advantage of certain significant connections between the material you have available to you and the solution you seek.

Organize your thinking as you would an equation. Set up an x as the unknown and manipulate the relationships of the facts until you can isolate and identify the x. Posit the solution to your problem as an unknown cause whose effects are showing themselves to you in your material. Posit the solution as an unknown effect of apparent causes contained in your material. Follow both paths through every level and down every detour and alternate route. The chain of causation may produce your solution.

Toy with cause and effect; reverse them and see what happens. Sequences can deceive. Because something appears to happen at an earlier time, you cannot assume it is a cause for what comes later.

John Stuart Mill developed five canons concerning cause and effect. They may help you in your reasoning.

1. Method of agreement: cause or causes that appear each time an effect occurs are true causes.

2. Method of difference: causal relation exists if a possible cause is present when a phenomenon occurs and absent when it does not occur.

3. Method of agreement and difference: two or more negative occurrences (suspected cause absent and effect being studied absent).

4. Method of residues: subduct from any phenomenon such part as is known by previous inductions to be the effect of certain antecedents, and the residue of the phenomenon is the effect of the remaining antecedents.

5. Method of concomitant variations: if an increase in A always

accompanies an increase in B, then A and B are causally related.

Regardless of which one or more of the approaches you take—brainstorming, classification, cause and effect—here is a suggestion that will make your preparation easier: it is a good practice to write down the problem at the beginning and to continue to write down your ideas as they occur.

Forcing yourself first to write the problem down succinctly and precisely clarifies your thinking and focuses your concentration in the right direction. Without a clear definition of the job before you, you may waste hours of needless work skirting the issue or running in place. You should write your ideas down to prevent them from being lost.

You gain an added dimension by putting space between you and your thoughts. Seeing your ideas leading an independent existence in black and white gives you a better perspective on them and shows off their interrelationship more clearly.

By this time you may be wondering what connection the law could have with the ideas of this chapter. Lawyers are not the only ones who organize their thoughts and think in different ways. But they have supplied the inspiration, because the ability to think in different ways is almost a question of survival for the practitioner. Lawyers, who have learned to expect the unexpected, prepare for any eventuality in the cases they handle and the functions they perform. Good attorneys must see all the possibilities, especially those that might cause problems. They must discover what could go wrong before the action begins. They need a sixth sense to draw out the implications beneath the surface.

Lawyers are especially fond of classification as a tool in preparing for any eventuality. The reliance on classification appears in the lawyers' dependence on checklists and forms. Checklists are available to guide them through the many procedures that contain numerous routine steps. Completing each step is easy but remembering each one can be difficult. Forgetting one step could spell disaster.

Any good law library has a healthy complement of formbooks. There are forms for virtually every common task the lawyer performs, including form contracts, pleadings, wills, articles of incorporation, and even form questions to ask in discovery. Legal problems have been classified to such an extent that the judgment of the lawyer is frequently needed only to measure the deviation of a particular situation from the general approach of a form.

Causation occupies an honored position in the law; it constitutes one of the basic elements of proof in any negligence case. It permeates the whole field of criminal law. Linking the person to the act, establishing motive, and proving the elements of a crime all rely on cause-and-effect reasoning.

While the law can claim no notable prominence in the use of brainstorming, the nature of the law as a system of predictions rewards the efforts of an attorney who can think in different ways and anticipate the factors that will decide where a certain course will lead. Broad, unfettered thinking places the good lawyer at an advantage.

Thinking in different ways also pays off when your goal is persuasion, but the process differs slightly. Allow your mind to roam freely collecting ideas and approach the job from many different angles just as you do when the problem consists of building a case. In building a case, though, you must return from the far points of your wanderings with the materials you have collected there to construct your case in the solid middle ground of the familiar and the conventional. Your excursion brings the strengths of broad thinking back into a narrower structure.

However, in persuasion, you fasten upon the most attractive remote location and settle there instead of returning to the center. The reason you remain off center when you seek to persuade is that people are interested in the differences in things, not the sameness of things, and are attracted by the unusual. If your message appears to be similar to what the majority is saying, people will not pay attention. People cannot be persuaded if they are not listening.

If you seem to be saying something different or if you are saying something in a different way, people will heed your message. The more surely you avoid the beaten path, the more likely is your message to gain attention, the more tempting your appeal will be, and the more easily you will persuade people of your position.

You can even appear logical in presenting your persuasive appeal from the singular position of your unique outpost. But being logical is definitely not all it is cracked up to be. Logic only cares that your argument is in a correct form and could not care less whether the conclusion is correct or substantial. You need only come forth with a rough facsimile of the standard forms and you can be as logical as anyone else.

There are only two forms—deduction and induction. Deduction means the conclusion follows necessarily from the reasoning. It is an argument from the general to the particular. In patterning your argument on the deduction model, you state your conclusion and back it up with the supporting evidence. After you present your evidence, you throw in a "therefore" for decoration and restate your conclusion.

Induction is an argument from the particular to the general. The conclusion can be either a general statement—a generalization —or a specific statement—a hypothesis. In either case you generalize beyond the specific instance you cite. To pattern your argument on the induction model, locate the problem, discuss the possible solutions, and finally pick the best one. Of course, you will be biased and your message will shine among the other alternatives.

Thinking in different ways from the defensive side of the line harkens back to the importance of expecting the unexpected and preparing for any eventuality. We call this posture negative thinking. You do not look on the bright side and await victory. You consider what could possibly go wrong and get ready for it to happen. Then, when something does go wrong, you can maintain your bearing and minimize its effect. When you treat a setback as minor, your opponent or an arbiter may perceive it as a minor point and give it less weight. Lose your poker face, and you may have to cash in your chips.

Your mind is a multifaceted instrument with an enormous capacity for creative problem solving from a variety of angles. Awaken this slumbering giant, and take advantage of the intricacy of your mind by thinking in different ways.

Chapter 14

Study Human Nature

Let observation with extensive view,
Survey mankind from China to Peru;
Remark each anxious toil, each eager strife,
And watch the busy scenes of crowded life.

—*Samuel Johnson*

When we do our homework, we set out in search of facts. The facts exist in some resting place before we seek them out; they wait there compliantly until we arrive. In our accumulation of facts, we acquire knowledge. Knowledge is stored. It is a commodity. It can be bagged, labeled, shipped from one to another, cut, weighed, and traded. Knowledge has great worth. It will repay the investment of a lifetime of study. But it is not enough. Knowledge is only a beginning.

In order to complete our development, we need savvy. Savvy is the street-smart, worldly wise wisdom derived from experience that lands us on our feet. Savvy sees the angles and knows how to play them. On its less respectable side it develops our craft, our cleverness, our cunning. But it also enlarges our compassion, our sympathy, and our humanity. Savvy understands how the machine is greased and who greases it. At the same time it understands human weakness and foibles and embraces people in spite of their shortcomings.

Savvy breeds in us an equanimity with the world and our place in it. We do not make excessive demands for perfection in people or situations. We gain the peace that a comfortable truce with frailty can bring. We understand more than we judge and accept more than we criticize.

As we develop our savvy, we learn to take the measure of a person, see behind actions to their significance, and discern motivations behind words. We understand what makes the other person tick and can predict with tolerable accuracy what course he or she will take and why. Armed with this degree of foresight and intuition, it would be a major upset if we did not hold our own; it would be a minor upset if our position did not improve.

A slight wrinkle appears when we arrive to pick up our portion of this wondrous savvy. It is not a durable good and cannot be passed from one person to another. Rather, it is a quality, transient in nature, which assumes different forms in different people.

It contains no answers that can be learned by rote. It is difficult to teach because it really does not possess any answers at all. We learn it by example or by emulation. Savvy is like poetry. It is powerful, earthy, truthful, and pithy; and yet it remains elusive, open to interpretation, mysterious. As our savvy grows, we operate more on an emotional level than on a cerebral level. Savvy uses our head, but it lives in our guts.

So, how do we develop our savvy? We begin by practicing our powers of observation and by becoming sensitive to levels of meaning. We should project our feelings in an attempt to understand what the other person experiences. We should be reluctant to accept things at face value but explore the dynamics of the words and deeds that we see.

Observation encompasses sight and goes beyond it. Observing entails paying attention to what we see. The images do not dance fleetingly before our eyes; instead, they register on our brain, and we then perceive the import and the sense of the activity.

The power of observation will give us an edge from the start because many people have sunk into a robotlike routine in which they walk around in a dream for most of the time. If you are in that majority of automatons, get out no matter what kind of struggle it takes. As you fight to observe what is happening around you, your experiences will become richer and your life more gratifying as your savvy increases.

The main object of your observation will be human nature. By human nature, we mean the qualities in people that make them what they are and influence what they do. Human nature includes both how people behave and why they behave that way.

Just as the human form can be a thing of beauty in selected instances, the human substance—human nature—can provide an attractive and fascinating display. It may take some practice to appreciate them equally, but then the bikini at the beach draws an instinctual response that observing human nature cannot match. The study of human nature does cover many more dimensions, if not curves. The beauty of a well-proportioned form is like an ice cream cone compared to the full-course, gourmet feast of human behavior and its sources.

The study of human nature cannot pass as a science because it is so inexact. It deals in approximations, educated guesses, and less educated guesses. The laboratory is so vast and varied that observers find more meaning in the individual departures from the norm than in the general rules. One consolation as you plunge into the labyrinth of human behavior is that human nature remains the same. For all its intricacy, it has neither changed nor is it ever likely to change. Whatever advances you make in reading a man's actions or motivations will benefit you in future situations. The important thing is to take the plunge and sharpen your observation of people.

The savvy that comes from your study cannot be taught, as it is a product of your efforts to observe people closely and to empathize with their feelings by stepping into their shoes. But you can nudge along the development of your savvy by reading from the science of human nature—psychology. You will receive no answers from psychology, but it can supply helpful clues to human behavior which you can apply in your own studies of people.

Keep a firm grip on your common sense and extract only what seems to have a practical value for you. You do not have to be a scholar to get the job done. And if you never read a page of psychology, this deficiency will not prevent you from understanding how people act. The average con artist may well be a more accomplished student of people than the authors of psychology texts.

In your pursuit of savvy you should invite one particular traveling companion—a healthy skepticism. You need not be ashamed to be seen in its company. Skepticism only stands for caution and verification. Adopt a doubting state of mind: incline to doubt rather than accept what people say, the reasons they give you for what they do and the generosity of their actions. We are all basically selfish in the sense that we take care of ourselves first before we look out for the welfare of others. It is a natural fact and one that too many people feel they have to apologize for.

Even the well-developed idealism of the missionary can recognize and work within the primary concern of all people for themselves. A missionary understands that no one will listen to a salutary message on an empty stomach. While a healthy person can afford to be religious, the sick and suffering may curse God for His tolerance of their misfortune as often as they show a selfless acceptance of His design. His design remains divine as long as it does not interfere with their own ends.

Our innate selfishness is less evident once we satisfy our basic material needs. It is harder to spot but no less real. People whose selfish goal is the acquisition of power may seem quite unselfish in giving of themselves, their time, and their possessions for the benefit of others. They are creating IOUs that can be redeemed later in the quest of the selfish aim of gaining power. Once our material needs are met, our behavior becomes more complex, and our selfish motivations hide under a thicker camouflage. Social acceptance takes on importance. Selfish desires run parallel with socially approved outlets.

Our skepticism must now work overtime. We must bring a neutral critical attitude to our inquiries of human nature. Without the reluctance to believe that comes from healthy critical reservations, we will be led around by the nose time and time again. When we employ a skeptical, show-me attitude, actions and motivations that hold up under the glare of our inquiry will win a well-earned trust that means something.

Both the persuader and the negotiator who understand human

nature succeed. As noted earlier, the skill of interpreting human behavior is largely self-taught. You must aspire to unfold its mysteries yourself and persevere in this endless chase. A few hints may help you in your pursuit. People invariably believe the things that satisfy or further their own needs and wants, and so it is crucial to identify those needs and wants.

Studies in persuasion have established that the acceptance of your message depends on the amount of internal resistance it meets. When your message activates already existing desires or beliefs, your audience will do much of your work for you and will naturally gravitate to your position. However, attempts to convince that contradict entrenched desires or firmly planted attitudes face heavy odds. If you can diagnose your audience's desires, you want to shape your message to fit their characteristics as closely as possible. Call it the "Why, I'm just an old country boy myself" approach.

The renowned psychologist Abraham Maslow, in his book *Toward a Psychology of Being,* describes five levels of needs in people. Perhaps his treatment can provide a scheme for organizing your study of human behavior and give some insight into what motivates people. The five levels build on each other. Only after needs on a lower level are met will a person turn attention to the next level.

The first level consists of physiological needs such as food, water, and sex. These ensure the preservation of the species. The second level is the need for safety. When the physical needs of these levels are satisfied, people then seek love and affection, a sense of belongingness. At the fourth level is the need for esteem. A person becomes concerned with prestige and reputation and desires a sense of achievement. The highest level holds the need for self-actualization, which describes a person's urge to realize his or her full potential.

Notice that even at this highest level people center their desires on themselves. Not only are people naturally selfish, but it seems people must be selfish in order to realize their full potential. Something of a paradox exists here because people need to reach their own potential in order to make productive contributions to society and lend support to others.

People possess certain tendencies that enable you to persuade them more easily. People tend to accept rather than analyze and criticize. They are susceptible to fallacious arguments because they are prey to the powers of suggestion. People feel comfortable with symbols and abstractions and tend to avoid the rigorous thinking required in precise reasoning. They rationalize endlessly and tend to hold to conclusions based on prejudices and habit.

People's needs and wants determine their attitudes more than the truth or intrinsic value ideas may contain. Their emotions are the primary force that motivates their thoughts and actions. However, the ability to influence people also depends on their individual personality traits and intelligence. The more intelligent a person is, the harder it becomes to persuade him or her without dressing the appeal within a carefully constructed logical framework. Because someone is intelligent, though, does not guarantee that he or she will be savvy.

We have already seen the importance of analyzing the occasion involved in the persuasion and listed some factors that you should consider when studying your audience. If this reminder does not refresh your recollection, you may want to go over them (see p. 48).

If you have been fortunate enough to isolate the desires in your audience that you should work on, you then want to find an approach that will capitalize on them. Here is a rough outline that may help you organize your persuasive appeal.

1. As always, get the audience's attention. Humor, shock, pique, demand, or ask them to listen. Consider any means that will draw attention while keeping you in their good graces.
2. Articulate their desires in some fashion. You can spell them out or barely hint at them. Let the audience know you recognize their desires and can help fulfill them.
3. Tie your message to their desires as the solution to their searching. This is the most difficult and delicate step and should be carefully planned.
4. Describe the result of your answer. Paint them a picture of their benefits from the successful interaction of your message with their desires.
5. Issue a call to action. Ask them to accept your message or to

take any necessary action to complete the picture. Request that they do their part to bring about the result.

Studying human nature is no less valuable in a conflict situation. In unusual circumstances, you may win your opponent over to your point of view. But normally, the process that has placed you in adversary positions will have eliminated the grounds for persuasion. Those people you are able to persuade will not square off against you in a contest, as they are already on your side. This selection process produces a highly resistant strain of opponent.

The point you should derive from this miniature model of evolution is plain and simple. Never underestimate your opponents. Give them the benefit of every doubt. You should act on the premise that they know exactly what they are doing until they show you otherwise. Let them prove themselves to be easy adversaries, unworthy of your talents.

You may wind up working a little harder, but the outcome will be no worse for you because of your efforts. Consider the surplus energy expended as insurance against the real possibility that you might misjudge your opponent. You would find yourself in an unfortunate predicament if your hunch about your adversary was wrong and you were left without this insurance. You could lose a contest that you should have won.

When you respect your adversaries, you receive another benefit. Giving them all the credit they could possibly deserve will spur you on to the fullest preparation of your case and to the best performance that you are capable of. When you take your opponent for granted, you may find the preparation of a case tedious and boring, and, in fact, it becomes a dreaded chore. When you respect your opponent, you will operate with a nervous edge that will keep your job interesting while it raises the quality of your work.

Butterflies in the stomach can be a valuable nuisance: you are not comfortable, but neither are you sluggish. A slight nervous edge will keep you alert and warm to the task. Without this edge you could even lose to a weaker case. Do not underestimate your opponents. If you assess that your case is stronger and let up, your opponent might surge right by you. You may get overconfident or just relax too much, like the hare who loses to the turtle. Your concentration may desert you. You might even be unaware of a change; then after you are bested, you are left to wonder what went wrong.

So never underestimate your adversary. Worry a little; a few grey hairs will not slow you down. An elementary study of human nature seconds this conservative approach. You cannot rely on your adversaries to level with you. So presume that their apparent weakness or good nature hides an attempt to slip you up, just as you have to try to slip them up. In a conflict, that attitude is the only practical one.

The study of human nature is fun. It plays to our natural curiosity and social instincts. Look at how its disreputable cousin, gossip, thrives. Along the way you will meet quite a few characters who will entertain you with their eccentricities. You will observe the strength of character that makes people great. The show ranges from slapstick comedy, to villainy, to high drama. People-watching is as varied as the oceans—and no drier. People-watching affords a very high return on your investment and helps develop your savvy.

Chapter 15

Make a Record

A man said to the universe:
"Sir, I exist!"
"However," replied the universe,
"The fact has not created in me
A sense of obligation."

—*Stephen Crane*

You are calling the Omnipotent Power and Light Company. The experience seems both familiar and strange. It seems familiar because this is the fifth time you have called in the last two and a half months. It is strange because you are calling from a pay phone. You have taken refuge in a restaurant since that is the only way for you to get a hot meal. Unfortunately, the restaurant is not far enough from your home for you to have walked off your frustration.

You have dialed the number enough now so that you could probably do it in the dark, which is precisely what you would have to do if you were calling from home. You had been given assurances that the power would not be shut off; however, those assurances will not toast your bread, run your television, or refrigerate your perishables.

The trouble began when you received a bill from Omnipotent

that totaled ten times the amount of the usual bite. You could have left every electric gadget on all month for the bill they were asking you to pay. When you called the office, the clerk checked the records and said your account had been billed by mistake for the electricity used by a nearby light industry. You were told that they would correct the computer information and that you should not pay the bill because your next statement would reflect the correction of your account. Set at ease, your mind dropped the matter, although a powerless sense of foreboding began creeping up your back.

The next month's bill showed that the computer had corrected your account and billed you properly for the recent period. However, it was not thorough enough, because, under previous balance, the same whopping figure appeared. Angry, you put in another call to Omnipotent and explained the situation to another clerk who departed to check the records. You were again told to pay the usual amount as charged under current balance and forget about the erroneous previous balance, so you mailed your payment in the same day. But you were starting to feel nervous.

You could see that the machinery at Omnipotent was escalating the conflict. They did not wait until the next billing date, but sent you a third bill after only two weeks. Apprehension mixed with anger as you opened the envelope. The statement thanked you for your partial payment and chided you for letting the previous balance survive intact again. Politely yet firmly, the computer informed you that this was the last reminder and urged you to set the matter straight and come across with your payment.

Musing on the wonders of technology, you considered evening the score with a vicarious yank on the cold computer's cord, but you bided your time until you could speak with the supervisor of customer relations. This time you did not want to take any chances. You could feel your grip on events slipping; you wanted a boost from authority. When the supervisor answered, you blew off steam for a while and then presented your lengthening case history. You received assurance that the supervisor would personally attend to your problem and that you needed do nothing further. The supervisor promised that it would be cleared up immediately and thanked you for calling the problem to the attention of customer relations.

When you called a week later, you recoznized the voice of the customer relations supervisor; however, the supervisor did not remember your previous conversation until you sketched the traumas of your dealings with Omnipotent. This second call was to report that you held in your shaking hand a final computer notice threatening you with the direst consequences for your stubborn lack of cooperation. The supervisor, flustered, reassured you of your safety and apologized again for this upreceeded mix-up: your case had been researched and everything had been found in order.

You figured then that the supervisor knew the office procedures better than you did—you only prayed it was well enough. What more could you do?

This last conversation took place five days before Omnipotent delivered the knockout blow.

Variations of this modern horror story recur constantly. What else can you do? Keep a record. Make a record. Document your case, and do not rely on your memory or on the assurances others give you. Make notes about all conversations and the surrounding details. Ask for written confirmation of assurances offered you, and gather supporting evidence for your position. When the crunch comes, your word will not carry the day for you.

Many writers carry a notebook and pen with them at all times to record their observations and thoughts, but you do not have to equal their preparedness. A camera hanging around a camera bug's neck constitutes a permanent, added appendage. Photographers see so much of life through a lens that you wonder how much is left for them to experience. You do not have to match this obsessive drive to frame and freeze each moment on film, but you should selectively record and preserve facts, details, bits of conversation, and impressions that may become significant later on. You must use your judgment to predict what might be important.

You should record the background when you anticipate that a problem may arise, when there is a fair chance for error or for something to go wrong, or in any case where the stakes are high or important to you. If you diagnose these symptoms, you should write down what happens sequentially while it is still fresh in your mind. As new events occur and new facts come to light, note them as soon as possible.

The more importance an item assumes, the more detail you will incorporate in your summary. It helps to include direct quotes of striking or meaningful phrases word for word. Make sure you collect what lawyers call the foundation. Memorialize the setting: time, place, names, and positions of people involved, relationships, and purposes behind actions.

In the example about shutting off the electricity, you probably would not record your first phone call unless Omnipotent already had a reputation for inefficiency. But one practice that is always a good idea when speaking with a business concern is to ask for the name of the person handling your case and write that down. So often you wind up speaking with a different person each time. When you get the name, you can request the person already familiar with your case in further dealings or refer the new person to the named person for more information. Most important, getting the person's name raises his or her visibility in a faceless bureaucracy. You will always get better service when you flush out a person's identity because it makes him or her accountable; that is the kind of pressure that is understood and that gets results.

When the bill arrives, still incorrect after your phone call, you know the time for recording has come. You write down as much information as you can remember from the first call and have pen and paper before you as you place the second call. Do not attempt a verbatim transcript, but do make notes of key ideas and phrases. After the conversation is over, go back over what was said and fill in the significant facts.

Depending on the situation and the degree of your confidence in the outcome, you may want to send a confirming letter. The purpose of a follow-up letter is to express the understanding you reached during your talk and to preserve that understanding in a more permanent form. If the other party disagrees with your interpretation of the meaning of the call, presumably you will be contacted to straighten things out. You may want to make this presumption explicit: "If I do not hear from you, I will presume that my review of our conversation is accurate and that you acknowledge its accuracy." It is as simple as that. But remember to remain polite. You can always yell your head off later if politeness fails.

Also, depending on the particular case, you may desire a response giving written assurances of promises the other party made orally. It is really easy for a person to slip into assurances that everything will be set right without knowing it to be so or even without believing that it will happen. Maybe the other person simply wants to get rid of you. Maybe he or she is the sympathetic type who genuinely does not like to see others upset and unhappy. Maybe he or she has been trained by an employer to reassure the customer at the front end regardless of the problem. It is part of our nature to reassure others in distress. We will tell a critically injured person, "Everything's going to be all right. You're going to make it," right up to the time of death. It's part of the treatment. You do not say, "You're a goner," or "Boy, you are really in bad shape," no matter how obvious that may be.

Often assurances given in good faith will languish and die once the heat of the moment passes and other business absorbs a person's attention. It is easier to get written assurances at an early juncture in the case because most businesses, although inconsiderate, are sincere in their efforts to satisfy customers, and especially because they usually believe the problem will be resolved. Thousands of similar transactions go off without a hitch, so they jump to the dubious conclusion that it is as likely that your problem will return to normal as it is that the normal routine will continue running smoothly. When you anticipate a problem in its early stages of development and secure an assurance in writing, you have bought yourself a bargain.

One further tip concerning your communications with an adversary should help you out especially in rancorous or sticky dealings. The law presumes that a letter sent to the correct address with proper postage is received. To elevate that presumption to an established fact, you can use certified mail and request a return receipt. Whenever you send a letter asking for written assurances or conveying vital information in hard-nosed dealings, certified mail will confirm that the other party received it by providing a numbered receipt with a signature on it. Also, because it is so obvious, we will no more than mention the absolutely fundamental practice of retaining a true copy of all important correspondence.

On the remote possibility that your case winds up in court, here is a minor technical point you might like to know. All of your writings from your efforts to keep a record are admissible into evidence to support your case under an exception to the hearsay rule called past recollection recorded. Except for this provision, you could only testify from memory to as much of the events and conversations as you could recall. Under this provision, once your attorney establishes that you wrote these statements, that they were correct when written, and that you cannot recall the facts, the statements will be admitted into evidence as written.

A more valuable technical point is that any written assurances the other party sends you will almost certainly be admissible into evidence under another exception to the hearsay rule called admissions of a party opponent. While oral admissions are likewise admissible, it is much harder to deny the existence of a written admission.

However, most disputes never reach the courtroom; they are settled by the parties because of the expense, time, and hassle involved with court proceedings. Herein lies the most valuable function served by your documentation and any assurances you might have obtained. Settlements mirror the relative strengths of the parties. If you have a weak case, you could be 100 percent in the right and pocket little more than the consolation of your worthiness. It might just as well never have happened if you lack the proof.

When the other party sees that you can substantiate your claim, the tenor of your negotiations abruptly changes. Your adversary turns conciliatory, and the question under discussion converts from Whether? to How much? You must prepare your case as if you will end up in court every time or else you will have to go to court to fight for your due more than is necessary. Ironically, preparing thoroughly enough to withstand courtroom scrutiny acts like an immunization and drastically reduces the chances that you will ever get to court.

The time you spend documenting the case will probably exceed the time you spend on hold on the telephone if you do not document your case—but not by much. And there will be no comparison between the results of using the different methods.

Now that we have that under our belt, let us take the exercise one step further. From "keep a record," we proceed to "make a record." We progress from observer and chronicler of events to actor and author of events. While the idea behind keeping a record is to record what happens, the idea behind making a record is to influence what happens in order to build your case into a winner. You cannot convert a losing case into a winner, but you can aim at one sitting on the fence and knock it off into your domain.

Making a record tests your skill as a broken-field runner. You twist and turn to avoid being tackled by the facts and issues that favor your opponent while you cut and swing wide to pick up any friendly blockers who can clear your path to the goal. If you are discussing your opponent's issues, you are probably helping to make a record for the opposition.

Making a record involves a dual approach to a conflict. You are concerned with the present and the future. You argue with one eye on convincing your opponent or an arbiter of your position and, with the other eye, you watch the record you are creating with the intention of shaping it so that it will effectively support your future argument. Your ultimate interest is to win the war, and you must evaluate the individual battles along the way according to their impact on the final result. You might lose an argument but count the battle as a victory in spite of superficial appearances if it advances your war effort.

Attorneys are always conscious of the record they are making. The phrase *make a record* is used often and has its source in a rule of law. Appeal courts will not consider new arguments on appeal. Any argument not made at the lower level is deemed to be waived for purposes of appeal. If you do not make a record, you get a quick "good morning" from everyone and you find yourself out of court. Even though it is clear that the trial judge will decide the case on one central issue, the thorough attorney will add every colorable argument to make a record just in case. On a drunk driving charge, the validity of the tests, proper arrest procedures, and the constitutionality of the statute may be argued as well as the main issue of the client's sobriety.

To illustrate the difference between keeping a record and making a record, let us cajole a child to bed at 8:00 P.M. If you were keeping a record, when 8:00 P.M. arrived, you would list the reasons why the child should cooperate. "It's 8:00 P.M., time for bed. You've had a nice evening. I let you watch television for an hour: I fixed you a snack; I read you a story. Now I expect that you will go to bed without a fuss." You have reviewed the *quid pro quo* for cooperation and the child may be grateful enough to cooperate. It is certainly better than a heavy-handed imperiousness that orders the child to obey. But the child may take a "what have you done for me lately" attitude and resist, because there is no present or future advantage. This approach fails to connect the past benefits with compliance.

If you were making a record, your argument would begin at 6:30 P.M. instead of 8:00.

6:30 P.M.: "If you cooperate at bedtime, I'll let you watch television for an hour."

7:30 P.M. "Remember that you promised to go to bed right away tonight. Because you're going to be good, I'll fix you a snack before you go to bed."

7:45 P.M. "It's bedtime. But I'm going to read you an extra long story and let you stay up a while longer because you promised to go straight to bed."

You have offered the same benefits, but you have tied them to future behavior in advance. Making a record envisions a certain approach to a conflict in which you prepare for the main event well in advance and guide the preliminary circumstances so that you improve your chances in the main event.

Why should you document your case and make a record in advance? Because you need support for your case; you need evidence to back up your claim. The Bible teaches that Jesus Christ performed miracles to deliver His message. Do you expect that people will accept your assertions on faith alone? People cannot be told. They have to see things for themselves. Not only will they not take something on another's word, but they should not accept another's assurances that something is so. The role of evidence is to enable another to see the validity of your assertion.

"Your honor, I am convinced that my client Ellen is innocent. Take my word for it, I just know she has done nothing wrong. You have to acquit her because she is not guilty, believe me." We would laugh at any lawyer who dared such a ludicrous presentation. No less than the professional advocate, you must offer proof to substantiate your claim.

The old professor, Aristotle, identified two essential elements of proof: the statement of the contention and the support for the contention. In addition to evidence, you can use logic to support a contention. We have already discussed the logical methods—induction and deduction, cause and effect, and analogy. The other form of support is evidence. There are five distinct categories of evidence: facts, opinions, examples, illustrations, and statistics. If you remember the categories, you can use them as a checklist to make sure that you have gathered all the support available for your argument.

A fact is a true statement or actual event. If a fact is not recognized by common experience (the sun rises in the east) or easily observed (he sneezed), you should have sources ready to cite as corroboration. An opinion is a judgment or belief that something is true. It falls short of knowledge but goes beyond an impression. Opinions can emanate from persons in authority, persons with expertise, or persons with experience. You can offer your own opinions as support for your argument if you can show that you qualify because of your experience or expertise to give an opinion on the subject. You should be able to identify your expert or authority and establish his or her credentials. For any opinion, you should be able to supply the basis for the opinion— the factors considered and the reasons causing the source to hold the opinion.

An example is a particular instance taken from the whole to show the character of the whole. It is a specific case that supports a general rule. An illustration is a particular instance separate from the whole which elucidates the whole graphically. An example consists of a sample from the whole while an illustration uses an exhibit or model to copy the whole. To exemplify a car, you would have to show a genuine car; to illustrate a car, you could show a photograph or a plastic model of a car. Examples must derive from the subject matter of your argument and have substance; that is, factual roots. Illustrations must be relevant to your argument and can be imaginary. In order to illustrate your point, you can travel beyond the facts to hypotheses. You can hypothesize to describe how a certain idea would work in practice or how a fictional entity operates.

Both examples and illustrations possess a special kind of power. They reduce the complex to the simple, transform the abstract into the concrete, clarify difficult material by enlisting the visual faculties of the listener, and add color and interest to dull material. Few arguments are strong enough that they will not benefit from the captivating change of pace of an example or an illustration. Use them freely to make your arguments more simple, concrete, visual, and interesting.

The fifth and final type of evidence is statistics, the science of frequency and probability of occurrence. It is a form of inductive argument using numbers to measure the frequency of occurrence of some event in order to find significance. Statistics is the systematic compilation of facts, instances, or events in order to predict the probability of future occurrences or the frequency of present occurrences beyond the sample. It is a form of inductive argument because it moves from the particular to the general, from the tested sample to the untested population or total group. Numbers function like adjectives; they describe and limit.

Statistics are tricky critters. They would rather mislead you than lead you. The famous quote attributed to Disraeli by Mark Twain is obligatory in any discussion about statistics: "There are three kinds of lies: lies, damned lies, and statistics." Any one of many variables that must be correct could easily and unobtrusively be wrong. For example, two out of three people who have tried Musty after-shave lotion like it best. My brother and my cousin were impressed; my wife was not. Or, two out of three randomly selected people preferred Musty. But to what? The third guy said he would rather use the kerosene.

You cannot be too wary of statistics cited to you, as they almost always sound more impressive than they have a right to be. Maybe our deferential respect for science and scientific methods carries over to statistical demonstrations.

Statistics give us the authority of an expert without the expense or effort. They naturally lend credence to our argument, and it is lamentably easy work to fashion them to suit our purposes. Why do statistics appear so often in advertising? They are effective. Why should you include statistics in your appeals? For the same reason. Besides, not one lawyer chosen for our survey denied the importance of statistics. (And those surveys should be mailed out to them soon.)

Once you have assembled all the support you need from logic and from the five categories of evidence—facts, opinions, examples, illustrations, statistics—you can ice the cake by adding one more feature to your argument. Lawyers call it the rationale, or the underlying reason why the listener should accept your argument. Ideally, it should cement the relationship between the evidence you offer to support your argument and the argument itself. It should explicate the progression from support to contention, showing it to be a proper and accurate step.

Often, the rationale turns out to be a high-sounding and vague appeal to emotion. Countless decisions in the law state that the rationale behind the result is public policy, the general welfare, or encouraging upright behavior. You could puzzle endlessly over the supposedly obvious connection between the result and the platitude in some cases. However, the principle endures heavy abuse because a rationale gives the audience a focal point that unifies your presentation. In effect it attaches another basis for people to accept your argument. The rationale provides an opportunity either to tie your presentation together or to ornament it with high-flying rhetoric.

In collecting your evidence and choosing a rationale, remember your audience. You want to select evidence in support of your arguments that appeals to the specific characteristics of your audience. We return again to the importance of analyzing the audience and the occasion. Use the motives, desires, values, and prejudices of your listeners. Study the occasion of your persuasion or conflict. What is the purpose of your argument? What should your evidence accomplish? How can you shape your evidence to capitalize on the characteristics of your audience so that your argument will be attractive to them?

You need support for your case. Gather the evidence that buttresses your arguments thoroughly. Make and keep a record. Document your position. Get it in writing. The Statute of Frauds, one of the dustiest precedents the law honors, was enacted as a safeguard against deception. Certain transactions were so important that a writing would be required as evidence because the effects of fraud would be so devastating. Included were contracts for the sale of land, promises in consideration of marriage, promises to answer for another's debts, and contracts for the sale of goods of a certain value.

The Statute of Frauds shows the law's concern for documentation. The practical sense that led to the law survives and flourishes to this day. Enact your own statute of fraud. When you decide that a transaction is important or could create a problem, document your position from the beginning. Collect the evidence that backs up your claim. Then you will be secure in the knowledge that you are fully prepared for any conflict that may develop.

Chapter 16

Put It in Play

Our doubts are traitors and make us lose the good we oft might win, by fearing to attempt.

—*William Shakespeare*

Ann Dodge has a wonderful family. Her dependable and affectionate husband, Herb, provides a comfortable living with his solid accounting position. Their three school-aged children are healthy, reasonably obedient, and self-reliant. The Dodges, who live in a pleasant residential tract, may not be a typical family in these changing times, but they fit the traditional image of an average American family, but for the lack of a cat or dog.

Ann leads a full life, as she rushes through her household duties of cleaning, cooking, shopping, and chauffering with minimal devotion in order to pursue the interests that are important to her. She works with the children to encourage their own developing interests and volunteers her time regularly at a nursing home and for special projects. She also holds a key political position in the local precinct.

She manages the family's active social life, entertains Herb's business associates, is active in charity drives, and is an easy mark for requests for help at school. She also plays bridge and tennis with Herb and her friends. She likes to read and stays well informed because of her preference for current nonfiction. Most notably, she takes business courses in the evening at the community college.

Only traces of defensiveness appear when Ann calls herself a housewife. She is not a full-fledged liberated woman—it is too late for her—but she has progressive attitudes and holds strong opinions on a few feminist issues. Her pleasant existence blocks any potential radicalism. Besides, she feels not in the least trapped by circumstances, only a little confined. And she genuinely enjoys life, although she will confess during the slower moments that she is not at peace with herself and that fulfillment has eluded her.

Ann Dodge has a treasured desire in that she would like to open a mail order business. Her talents, common sense, and business studies all verify the merits of the idea. Her chances for success are good; a bonanza is plausible. She has extensively researched the market and investigated the competition. She has mastered the rules of the game and thoroughly prepared her operation. She has done her homework.

The fact that she has not begun her business does not bother her, but the realization that she probably never will troubles her no end. The size of the fight to make the business a success would pale in comparison with her uphill battle against a lifelong pattern of deference. Because she was not supposed to be aggressive, she deferred to the needs and preferences of others. Habitual deference has robbed her of the bone-tough confidence required in her venture.

She shies away from recognizing the ability buried within her to meet a challenge and act on her dream. Deference prevents her from testing her mettle and gaining the experience of her attempts. Chronic doubt has filled the void, and because she has never tried, she has come to believe that she cannot.

You must surmount the crest of the hill and convert preparation into action. Research and investigation are essential, but reflection must give way to action. Confidence must supplant doubt. Doubts are a sign of healthy preparation, but they can also cripple your performance once the action begins. In preparing your position, you face your doubts, investigate their basis, judge their impact, and resolve them as best you can. If a doubt ripens into a substantial reason for refraining from the action, fold your hands and wait for the next deal.

However, err on the side of boldness, because inclinations tip toward timidity. Unless you can see a good reason for not acting, put it in play. If Ann Dodge approached her tennis the way she did her business idea, she would never serve the ball. Her mind would be preoccupied with double faults, foot faults, and smashing returns.

Murphy's Law holds: If anything can go wrong, it will. Our variation on Murphy has it that if you think of the things that can go wrong, more of them will. When doubts absorb your mind, you create the climate for defeat. A negative outlook produces inferior results.

Belief in yourself and in your endeavors is a powerful and effective quality. A healthy ego and confidence in your performance will almost magically disperse those nagging blunders and "bad breaks" that doubt introduces. Why permit doubts to assail your actions when you have done your homework? Even worse, why let doubts stop you from converting your preparation into action? You would waste all the time and efforts of your preparation. It would be a shame to work so hard getting ready only to balk when the moment for action arrives.

The lawyer is a good example of the practice of putting it in play. If anything, a lawyer may rush to the battle too quickly. It is difficult to practice law without a well-developed ego. A lawyer who lacks confidence in his or her case or in the ability to win it does not adequately represent the client. Neither will this lawyer last long in the competitive arenas of courtroom and conference room.

The successful business executive also exemplifies the willingness to act. Three characteristics distinguish the good executive: the ability to judge present conditions, to predict future trends, and most important to make decisions once the facts and figures are assessed. The ability to make decisions signals a propensity to move from preparation into action and shows an action orientation.

Just as mosquitos do not dissuade you from camping, mistakes should not prevent you from acting. Like the mosquito for the camper, mistakes will appear wherever your action takes you.

But preparation reduces errors to the status of a minor irritation. A mistake represents an opportunity to learn in the long run just as much as it constitutes a setback in the short run.

Since mistakes are universal, the edge goes to those who learn from their errors. If you view errors as lessons to guide future actions, you will not repeat your mistakes but only make new ones and smaller ones. Even if you are afraid of making a mistake, you might as well act anyway, because not acting is the biggest mistake you can make. If you wish to gain the wisdom that only experience can supply, join the fray.

Put it in play. When inexperience and doubts threaten your initiative, ask yourself this question: Does the lack of sexual experience justify celibacy?

Chapter 17

Determine the Burden of Proof

. . . the best test of truth is the power of the thought to get itself accepted in the competition of the market.
—Oliver Wendell Holmes, Jr.

You live in an apartment building and like to stay up late at night. You play your stereo at high volume because you believe that music must penetrate to your bones for full appreciation. The tenant below you, a disciple of Ben Franklin, is that wise type of bird who thinks it healthy to collect a wealth of early worms. He objects to your concerts staged in the middle of the night.

You reply that 11:00 P.M. is barely the beginning of the night, much less the middle. He complains to the manager, citing a clause in the leases where the tenants agree "not to make or permit any disturbance, noise, or annoyance whatsoever detrimental to the premises or to the comfort and peace of any of the inhabitants of said building or its neighbors."

The manager has scheduled a meeting with you, but before you plunge into combat with your neighbor, you should put the conflict in perspective. In order to identify both the starting point of the conflict and the framework that the arguments should follow, you need to determine the burden of proof. We use the phrase "burden of proof" to describe two related concepts.

One can also be called the standard of proof. The standard of proof measures the amount of evidence required to establish the truth of an argument in the type of conflict presented. This is the ordinary meaning of the phrase "burden of proof" in the law. Examples of standards of proof from the law include the preponderance of the evidence (a win, however slight the margin); the manifest weight of the evidence (a comfortable margin); clear and convincing evidence (a large margin); and beyond a reasonable doubt (a rout, a laugher).

The standards of proof reflect the gravity of the case, how much is at stake, and the consequences of losing. They recognize human fallibility and thus demand greater certainty for more serious proceedings. The arbiter must be sure beyond a reasonable doubt before labeling the accused a criminal and revoking liberty. The meaning of beyond a reasonable doubt is self-explanatory. Preponderance of the evidence, the usual standard in civil cases, means that an argument is more probably true than not true.

The other concept included in the burden of proof is known also as the burden of persuasion. The burden of persuasion singles out which party must go forward with the evidence. It fixes on the person who has to initiate the case. Knowing where the burden of persuasion falls is indispensable in planning the strategy of your argument. There is an ocean of difference between the other person having to prove that you did something and your having to prove that you did not.

If nothing happens, if no evidence is introduced, or if the evidence introduced by each side balances, the person with the burden of persuasion loses and the person without it wins. While the standard of proof remains the same throughout the proceedings, the burden of persuasion may shift back and forth between the contestants: "The complainant says this, so how do you respond?"

The person who has the burden of going forward with the evidence does not have to prove his or her case, shoot down the opponent's case, and come away a clear winner all at once. The burden requires the establishment of what is called a *prima facie* case, or one strong enough to win a decision on the issue in dispute unless the other side can contradict or explain the evidence.

So the burden of persuasion is the obligation resting on a party to establish a *prima facie* case or to refute a *prima facie* case established by the adversary, depending on the state of the dispute. Once one party has met the burden of going forward with the evidence, the burden shifts to the other side to present evidence refuting or explaining the first party's evidence. If the second party is successful, the first party must refute or explain the second party's evidence, and so on.

You should examine both concepts contained in the burden of proof before you begin the fight. Normally, the burden of persuasion or of going foward with the evidence lies with the person who brings the case or makes the complaint. The usual standard of proof approximates the preponderance of the evidence.

In our example about the loud stereo, the complaining tenant would have the burden of persuasion. The standard of proof would fall somewhere along the spectrum between preponderance and manifest weight. The reason for the need for a wider margin in the example is that the parties do not start out on an equal footing. The other tenant is trying to roust you from your apartment, and this interference with your property rights demands a stronger showing than a preponderance. It is not enough to say, "It is more likely true than false that you play your stereo too loud too late at night."

The standards of proof listed are categories used in the law. Your analysis does not need to be limited to these categories, but they can provide a guide for your thinking. Judge the particular conflict you face independently and carve out your own standard of proof to fit the specific case. Consider the factors mentioned before (the gravity of the case, how much is at stake, the consequences of losing), as well as the relationships of the parties and the arbiter, the effect of a decision either way on all concerned, attitudes and values, motives, and the like.

Look for the presence of presumptions that might influence the burden of proof. The legal presumption of innocent until proven guilty places the burden of persuasion on the prosecution to prove the guilt of the accused. Because everyone is presumed to know the law, you will not defeat a *prima facie* showing of your liability by explaining that you did not know that the applicable law existed. When you sign a document, the presumption is that you have read it, understand it, and agree to be bound by its provisions.

You can overcome presumptions by introducing contrary evidence. Presumptions are creatures of convenience that enable our transactions to run smoothly. They are not commandments written in stone. However, you should locate any presumptions operating in a particular case because they will do a job on you if you do not work on them.

For example, the apartment manager might presume that your tastes run to the blare of rock music if you are young and have long hair. If the manager disdains rock music, he may automatically sympathize with the complainant, project his feelings into the dispute, and lower the complainant's burden of proof. If your listening habits favor Mozart and Debussy, you want the manager to know that. Now, if the manager has a thing about this long-haired music, too, you really have a dilemma.

A look at debating may crystallize understanding of the workings of the burdens of proof at the same time as it offers you hints on how to satisfy the burden of persuasion. In a debate the standard of proof is the preponderance of the evidence, and the burden of persuasion resides with the affirmative side. The negative side wins the debate when the affirmative cannot establish a *prima facie* case or when the evidence balances.

The essential parts of the affirmative case are simple. They must proceed with evidence that reveals a need for a change and demonstrates the benefits to be gained by the proposed change. They may also anticipate the negative case and offer defensive arguments answering likely objections to their position. When you meet a situation in which you have the burden of going forward with the evidence, consider using the quick one-two punch of need for change and benefits gained to satisfy the burden of persuasion.

The negative case affords more leeway. After the affirmative offers a *prima facie* case, and the burden of persuasion shifts to the negative side, the proponents of the negative can choose from among five basic responses. First, they can argue the opposite of the standard affirmative case. They show a need for the status quo, or at least a lack of need for change, and the benefits derived from leaving things undisturbed.

The next four responses attack the affirmative's proposal for change, "the plan." Second, aim at every point the affirmative makes, criticizing each step of the proposal. Third, aim at one pivotal point underpinning the entire proposal and attack it in depth. Fourth, agree with one or two innocuous points of the proposal to show your fair-mindedness and attack the rest. Fifth, point up the inadequacy of the affirmative's plan by offering a better one of your own.

You should recognize an important theme implicit in our treatment of the burdens of proof. Procedure plays a vital role, not only in setting the scene and acting it out, but also in contributing to the final outcome of a conflict. The format of the argument often surpasses the substantial points raised in its amount of influence bearing on the decision.

An outstanding example of the power of procedure to govern the results of a case is the use of delay as a strategic tool. If your opponent has the burden of going forward with the evidence, and you delay the argument of the case until the issue becomes stale or fades away, then you win. You have won your argument by not arguing.

You will be surer of success and hassled less when you can prevent the conflict from being joined than when you must refute your adversary's position in cases where he or she has the burden of persuasion. For example, if you can put off the confrontation about the stereo with the manager and the other tenant until the tenant's lease expires, the other tenant may just decide to move out to quieter quarters.

In addition delay is one of the few effective responses in a case where you are heading toward defeat. (The other responses—confusion, compromise, and exaggeration—will be discussed more elsewhere.) A losing case never argued becomes a tie, and when you tie a losing case, you have earned a victory. Thus, delay can turn a losing case into a small victory.

The criminal defense lawyer, confronted with a stable of prosecution witnesses with strong testimony implicating the client, fights a war of attrition. He or she crawls through pretrial hearings and conferences, canceling meetings to the limit of credibility. He or she drags out pretrial discovery with added depositions and requests for clarification of material. The pièce de résistance comes at trial time. He or she piles excuse upon excuse to seek the maximum number of continuances. The goal is to deplete the resources, patience, and fervor of the adversary.

Each time a witness appears for nothing his or her resolve weakens. He or she wonders if his efforts are futile. Frustration and expenses grow, and he or she may decide the imposition is no longer worth it. Each desertion improves the defense's chances and creates greater doubts among the remaining witnesses about the value of their own continuing sacrifices. Even if enough witnesses persevere to convict the accused, the defending lawyer has kept his or her client out of jail a longer time and has probably reduced the sentence by dulling the impact of the case.

Evasion, the subtle flight from relevance and materiality, is a good tactic for advancing the strategy of delay. When you are asked a yes-or-no question, you answer yes and no and launch a long, rambling explanation of your conclusion. Evasion is a blood brother to confusion and distraction. There is a lot of overlap between them. When you are asked a question to which you do not know the answer and you cannot think of a colorable evasive answer, you should begin an evasive monologue on the question.

Politicians do this all the time. It goes something like this: "That's a good question and I'm glad you asked it. It shows how perceptive you are, and I admire your interest in this subject. The question deserves an answer and that is why I'm talking right now." [I'll never admit this to you but I don't happen to know the answer to your question, or I do, but it's terribly painful and embarrassing to me.]

"Rather than responding to it either directly or indirectly, let me pose another question of my own which is somewhat related to your question and which should also interest you." [I am fully prepared to answer my question brilliantly to show you how responsive and deserving I am, and I hope that the questions are similar enough and my brilliant answer is long enough so that you will not notice the discrepancy.]

Your long, involved answer should lend support to the saying "Time heals all wounds." And if you can keep the discussion sidetracked, your efforts could justify a paraphrasing: Time wounds all attempts to heal.

Note that delay as a strategic tool is far removed from inaction. The use and power of delay does not contradict the principle of putting it in play. You are doing nothing. You take action, except that your action promotes the status quo of the case.

Call it active delay, if you like, to keep the distinction between delay and inactivity. Sometimes, the alternative to going forward with a dispute—delay—is preferable to proceeding. Your defensive work in detaining a case through delay can demand just as much energy and return just as great a reward as your thoughtful and exhaustive preparation for arguing a case.

Several principles of persuasion pertain to the standards of proof and the power of delay. Not surprisingly, the effects of a persuasive attempt tend to wear off in time. Delay between your opponent's presentation and your rebuttal can work to your advantage for this reason. While your message is fresh, your opponent's may have faded into the distance.

In order to increase the life of your message if you are fighting delay, you should liberally employ repetition and active listener participation at the time you deliver your message. Repetition and active listener participation are strong assets in any case because of the tendency of persuasive attempts to wear off. While the effects of persuasion gradually dim, the manifestation of the effects of persuasion often appears some time after the message arrives rather than immediately. There seems to be a period of incubation while the message works on previous beliefs before the influence of the message is evident.

One of the most difficult standards of proof to satisfy is called abuse of discretion. Abuse of discretion is a common standard of proof in the law for cases on appeal. The party appealing must establish that the decision of the trial judge constituted an abuse of discretion. Members of the appellate court are not about to reverse one of their judicial brothers just because it looks like the judge was wrong. They will bow to the original judgment, saying that the judge saw things firsthand and had a better opportunity for observing and considering all factors. They will not substitute their judgment for the first decision, and they give the first judge wide latitude. For reversal, the judge must have been blatantly wrong or must have clearly violated broad discretion.

Use the phrase *abuse of discretion* to jar your memory about the burdens of proof and the power of delay. You have the discretion to study your case to discover the standard of proof needed. You have the discretion to study your case to determine who has the burden of persuasion, the duty to go forward with the evidence. You have the discretion to use delay strategically to improve your position. You abuse your discretion if you ignore the advantages of this analysis and approach.

Chapter 18

Demand a
Proper Foundation

*Is it shocking to put a definition or rule of law in such a naked
form as to show that it completely begs the question? It should
not be so; for what often seems to be our favorite method of
legal argument is to beg the question in complicated and repeti-
tious terms.*

—*Arthur Linton Corbin,*
Corbin on Contracts

Law school could be renamed approach school, because it
teaches a way of thinking—a way of dissecting a fact pattern and
of analyzing its significance. The mastery of substantive law takes
on a lesser role. Law students learn how to think more than they
learn what to think.

The first exercise law students attack is briefing cases. After
deciding a case, a court will issue a legal opinion—a narrative
describing the facts, citing applicable precedents, and delivering
the judge's decision and the reasons behind it. A brief of this
opinion breaks the narrative down into its main component parts
and extracts the vital points of the analysis.

The brief begins with a summary of the key facts of the case
followed by a statement of the issue, in the "whether or not" form,
which the case presents for resolution. Next is the rule of law, the

guiding general principle based on enumerated statutes or previous cases or both. Then what is termed the holding of the case applies the rule of law found in the precedents to the facts of the instant case and comes up with a decision. Finally, the brief concludes with the reasoning behind the decision including any particular rationale. Facts, issue, rule of law, holding, reasoning— before they are finished, students will repeat this analysis and extraction hundreds upon hundreds of times in their legal briefs.

The brief symbolizes the analytical approach law training takes where nothing can be taken for granted, nothing left to chance, and nothing assumed. Law students must scrutinize every sentence and each word. They must select the wheat from the chaff and the material from the immaterial. They must separate what is paramount from what only sounds important or from the interesting irrelevancy. Later, as lawyers, they will win or lose cases depending on how well they developed this judgment.

This approach sharpens critical faculties, but it also breeds a tendency to doubt. With such a background, lawyers naturally build up a large amount of skepticism. They will not accept a statement or a claim unless credible evidence supports it. They require the laying of a proper foundation.

This chapter focuses on the reliability of information. The posture is defensive. When someone tries to sell you a product, an idea, or an opinion, how will you break through the sales pitch to judge the merit of the claim? When you are arguing with someone, how can you throw up obstacles that block the advance of that position?

You want to develop a "show me" attitude, sometimes as a neutral method of verifying the accuracy of another's claim, and sometimes as an artifice to make an opponent's job tougher. If there is a sucker born every minute, that is an accident of birth. If we neglect to sharpen our critical powers and allow another to sucker us because of our haphazard analysis, we have no one else to blame. If we do not offer resistance to an adversary by demanding the laying of a superabundant foundation, or a proper foundation at the least, we will find ourselves on the short end more often than necessary.

If we demand a proper foundation, then we require an adversary to authenticate a claim by producing substantial, relevant evidence. We will not accept information unless its reliability can be demonstrated. We will probe and analyze the case, looking for logical fallacies or unjustified leaps to conclusions. When we find weaknesses, we will expect our adversary to overcome them rather than gloss them over.

Our search for relevance insists not only that the supporting evidence for a claim has a solid connection with the claim but also that it has probative value; that is, it must logically tend to prove the claim it supports. Relevant evidence relates to and proves a claim.

A good advocate will settle for no less than a proper foundation for opposing assertions. Allowing the other side to offer unsubstantiated claims lightens its burden and makes your arguments seem weaker in comparison. An unbending resistance to any argument not supported with a proper foundation will at the least assure that the burdens on each side in the contest are equal. More likely, it will give you an advantage because the average adversary you tangle with will not be especially vigilant in detecting all of your unfounded assertions.

You can almost certainly gain the advantage by forcing your opponent to define terms even where no clear definition is possible. We are all susceptible to requests for definition because we have learned that we do not know the meaning of words or concepts that we cannot define, and we believe we should not discuss a subject if we cannot define the terms involved. However, there are concepts and terms that do not admit of clear-cut definition. Other concepts and terms are capable of definition but are so complex that an attempt to define them on the spot would lead to distortion.

For example, you consider an acquaintance from work a crashing bore, and you would like to stuff a few of his inflated opinions down his throat. At an office party, you meet in front of a sculpture of a man and woman intimately entwined. Since you have nothing in common, your conversation turns to the sculpture. He labels it obscene and launches a fine arts lecture. You edge in with your opinion that it is a work of art, not because you think so, but in order to bait him with the position on the other extreme.

Now you are both vulnerable to a request for definition. Whoever takes the offensive and presses the other to define *obscene* or *work of art* should prevail in the clash because either term is difficult to define and will cause insurmountable problems to the one cornered into attempting ready definitions.

Once you induce an opponent to define complex, abstract, or erudite ideas or words, you have him or her on the run, in danger of fabricating definitions that correspond to nothing in fact, and in danger of looking foolish in an unwise attempt to define. An unexpected request for definition may even confuse or disconcert an adversary. Assertiveness may follow composure out the window.

Related to the request for definition is the confession of ignorance. You should certainly ask for an explanation of any part of your adversary's case that you do not understand. Do not be afraid to seem slow. Getting the information straight is most important, and you should ask for clarification continuously until you grasp everything clearly.

Sometimes, it pays to ask your opponents for explanations when you already know what they are trying to say. This is the device called the confession of ignorance. They may be struggling to explain their ideas clearly, and additional requests for explanation could confuse their presentation and draw them off track. You might also cause them to lose patience and act or speak impulsively, to their detriment. They may even contradict themselves.

The best contribution that asking for an explanation makes is to give you time to think. You can delay your response to an argument if you cannot think of what you want to say or how you should say it. Asking your foe for clarification of a position gives you the time to organize your thoughts and plan your rebuttal. After all, you have already heard the opposing position; so you do not have to listen to what is said but can concentrate on your own business.

We have already noted that logic is concerned with the correctness of argument, not the accuracy of its conclusion. Logic analyzes the relationship between the conclusion and its supporting evidence. The law has the identical concern when it measures the relevance of evidence against the issue in dispute. This is why good lawyers are good logical thinkers. When you demand the laying of a proper foundation for your opponent's arguments, you have the same concern. Evidence logically connected to the argument is required, and logic provides a helpful tool in your probe of your adversary's foundation.

Logical fallacies can sneak past you. They are subtle. If you miss a few, do not feel bad. Formal logic is overrated. Rather than studying its undistributed middles, and its concern with what happens when you affirm and deny the antecedent or the consequent, you should concentrate on a few general points. First, break arguments down into their parts. Outline the argument by converting it into simple declarative sentences or phrases. If you can express the ideas in a syllogism, so much the better. Use common sense. Stripped bare, does the argument hold together and make sense?

Second, assess materiality. Is all the supporting evidence relevant? Has other relevant evidence that weakens the argument been left out?

Third, watch for word manipulation. Convert abstractions into concrete terms, and resist loaded words that carry emotional charges.

Fourth, search for an unarticulated premise. An unarticulated premise is the proposition that underpins your adversary's argument but that is not expressed. Suppose a suitor offers the invitation, "Would you like to see my etchings?" He entices you at length. You break his argument down into its parts like this: My etchings are beautiful. Everyone who sees them enjoys them. You appreciate the finer things in life. You would enjoy seeing my etchings. Therefore, come into my parlor because you will enjoy it. The unarticulated premise is obvious. It has more to do with his enjoyment than yours: "If I can get her into my parlor, I can make my move." A popular term for the unarticulated premise now is the "hidden agenda."

Fifth, screen the assertions that make up the argument for an inconsistent logical extension. For example, a national politician says he is personally opposed to abortion and desires anti-abortion legislation. However, he believes this is a local issue and will take no positive action. The federal government should leave it to the states, he asserts.

This position is logically inconsistent, as the politician is dodging the issue. What is the significance of the difference in size between the federal government and a state on a question like abortion? There is none. If the issue were defense, the significance would appear. Extending the logic, the states should leave it to the cities and towns. The cities and towns should leave it to their members. Each citizen can decide the abortion issue for her own constituency: herself. Thus, any individual can choose to get an abortion. Therefore, the politician favors abortion on request.

When we analyze the question of the reliability of information, our goal is to limit our opponent to introducing only reliable information. In the law the rules of evidence developed in response to the need for reliable information, and the law distinguishes between direct and circumstantial evidence.

Direct evidence supports a contention directly, without an accompanying inference or presumption: I saw the defendant snatch that woman's purse. Circumstantial evidence supports a contention with the aid of an inference or presumption: the defendant, holding a woman's purse, ran past me and dashed into an alley. We infer that the defendant committed the unwitnessed crime. Maybe it was his wife's purse, and she was waiting in the alley for it. Any leap of logic required to arrive at our conclusion reduces the reliability of the evidence.

The rules of evidence require firsthand knowledge and exclude hearsay. Witnesses must have observed or experienced what they testify to and cannot pass on information obtained from others. Out-of-court assertions cannot be tested by cross-examination. When other factors substitute for cross-examination in safeguarding reliability, exceptions to the hearsay rule appear.

For example, a witness may relate what another said immediately before death under the exception to the hearsay rule called dying declarations. When the declarant senses impending death because of homicide, declarant's statement of facts concerning the homicide is admissible in a prosecution of the homicide. We want to discourage a party from improving the case by rubbing out damaging witnesses. Also, reliability is supplied by the declarant's knowledge that life is almost over.

Look for leaps of logic in what your adversary says. Does the evidence directly support the argument, or is it propped up with presumptions, implications, irrelevancies, and calls to emotion? Are the cards laid out on the table directly and simply, or are attempts made to hide an unarticulated premise?

Good lawyers attempt to impeach any witness whose testimony is not truthful. Impeach in this sense means to question the credibility of the witness. The rules of evidence allow impeachment for prior inconsistent statements; bias, interest, or hostility; bad conduct or poor reputation for truthfulness; and faulty perception or memory. These categories may help you check out an opponent.

Review these additional factors to see if you can challenge the reliability of your adversary's information. They can help you focus on the person as well as on the argument. Your opponent may not be the proper spokesperson for the assertion. For example, a son says to his friend, "My dad can beat up your dad." His father says, "My son enjoys helping me with the yard work." We should ask the father about the first statement and the son about the second.

Finally, we must consider the largest transgression against reliable information—the lie. Lies are often effective because of their boldness. As we guard against a subtle trick, the gross distortion slips by us. The best way to handle a lie is to label it as such, with more or less diplomacy depending on the situation. Arguing against a lie is a major job. It is better to label it, expose its inconsistency, and refuse to let it enter the dispute.

All of the tricks, pitfalls, irrelevancies, and fallacies we seek to prevent can be gathered under the heading of begging the question, which assumes as true that which must be proved. Laying a proper foundation represents the other pole. Begging the question is the extreme opposite of laying a foundation. "Accept my argument because it is acceptable. Believe me because I am credible." Well, saying does not make it so. You require adequate, relevant evidence in support of anyone's statement.

For an adversary, you become extra finicky. Nothing seems to satisfy you. Somehow your adversary's terms remain vague and need more definition, more explanation. Your adversary's evidence does not relate to the argument directly enough and never seems to prove the case sufficiently. You are so dumb you have to be shown what the argument is and how it can be supported, over and over. Dumb like a fox. You will be amazed at how someone as dense as yourself can give fits to your opponent and frustrate all attempts to establish the case.

Chapter 19

Develop a Theory
of the Case

*Much of my success as a trial lawyer lay in the fact that I was
always willing to give the opposing attorney six points in order
to gain the seventh—if the seventh was the most important.*
—Abraham Lincoln

"No matter what I do," complained Martha, "somehow it always
falls short of being acceptable to Paul's parents. They are always
friendly to me, at least on the surface. But they don't miss an opportunity to take subtle digs at whatever I do. Their compliments
invariably hide some double meaning and come across backhanded.

"Every change they notice somehow gets attributed to me, and
for the worse. If Paul puts on weight, I'm letting him go to seed.
If he looks thin, I'm neglecting him and not cooking properly.
When we don't see them as often as they would like, it must be
because my activities are taking up too much time and getting in
the way of our visits. If Paul has other plans, they understand how
a hard-working son needs his diversions."

Martha's friend interjected sympathetic nods and assents which
encouraged her outpouring to continue. "I'm not thin-skinned by
any means and could put up with that. But, on top of it, his
mother ceaselessly compares poor Paul's miserable life with me to
the idyllic piece of heaven she once provided him."

"I enjoy doing things for Paul. I don't mind doing the wash, but I'm not about to iron his underwear. I'm happy to slice a grapefruit and put it in front of him in the morning, but I'm not about to section the lousy thing for him and put a cherry in the middle. I'm tired of tales about how the now languishing Paul flourished under her care with moister chicken and more understanding."

Martha became angrier as she talked, thinking of examples of her grievance. "If they would come right out and criticize me openly, I would have a chance to defend myself. But the subtle sniping here and there is hard for me to counteract. And Paul doesn't make it any easier. He barely notices that it's going on. When I talk to him about it, he readily admits that they are overstepping their bounds, but he doesn't show much concern. Because he hasn't noticed how frequent their comments are and how much it bothers me, he shrugs it off with a hollow 'Don't let it get to you.' And I'm ready to blow up."

Martha has become bogged down by the specific details of her conflict. Her scope has narrowed to the particular insults she has suffered. This reaction is completely understandable and is easy to fall into. Yet, it is a reaction. The events of her conflict are moving her along and controlling her. She can no longer see the forest for the trees and needs to form a broader perspective of her difficulty. She should get a grip on the conflict and begin to act for her own benefit instead of reacting and remaining unhappy.

Her effort to get on top of the situation would begin nicely if she would develop a theory of the case. A theory of the case is an operating principle that is shaped from your analysis of the facts and your judgment about the likely results of various actions. The working blueprint of your strategy, it is the game plan that you evolve from the study of scouting reports and the assessment of the strengths and weaknesses of your team and your opponent.

Once you develop a theory of the case, you can more clearly see individual events in the light of a larger perspective. You can handle the problems located in the parts, because you see the overall picture. Instead of reacting to the immediate emotions of each incident, you can study the significance of the incident from the detached viewpoint of your theory of the case and act according to the incident's effect on the big picture.

Most people eventually generalize from their experience and learn a lesson or two. What you do when you develop a theory of the case is to project the eventual pattern before the case gets well underway. Like the news coverage of election returns, you look for trends and predict the outcome early. Then you interpret the tabulations as they mount according to the theory you have settled on.

While we prefer the full and balanced framework that a historical context supplies, we cannot wait until events have passed us by before acting on them. For our purposes, hindsight is as worthless as it is accurate. We settle for the imperfect perspective of an immediate setting and forego the complete appraisal of a historical context, which has greater accuracy but much less value.

Suppose Martha were to develop a theory of the case. Her focus has been on the instances where Paul's parents criticized her. She has felt hurt because she has rationally evaluated her treatment of Paul, justified it, and resented the higher, altered standards imposed by his parents.

Instead, she should concentrate on the causes of their behavior. The behavior is a symptom. Paul is their youngest child and the last to leave home. Remnants of the attention he received as the baby of the family stubbornly persist, and his parents find it hard to let go. With an empty house, they now face a transitional point in their own lives. After years of child care, the adjustment to other interests is difficult.

It still will not be easy for Martha to put up with their carping, but developing a theory of the case can help her cope with it. She can realize that Paul's parents are not attacking her but are expressing their own problems. She need not feel threatened or defensive by their comments because she understands that she is not their target. They are fighting their loneliness and fear of their own uselessness, not her.

In developing a theory of the case, we must decide what is really important. We must separate the things of importance from those things that only seem important but that we can safely ignore. In judging the primary issues in a conflict, in selecting our arguments, in choosing the means of persuasion, and in budgeting our attention and time we must assign priorities. Assigning priorities is the nuts and bolts of the job of developing a theory of the case.

We owe a lasting debt to the late Italian economist Vilfredo Pareto for the insight expressed in Pareto's Law, which states that the significant items in a given group normally constitute a relatively small portion of the total items in the group. An effective theory of the case highlights that small portion of significant items while it allows the other trappings to settle into the background.

We can paraphrase Pareto's Law by saying that a small portion of our energies accounts for the greater part of the results that we achieve. By giving priority to the few significant items, we can concentrate our energies on that small portion of efforts that yields the highest return. There is something of a trade-off between emphasis and all-inclusiveness. Remember that we stated earlier that the positions of emphasis for arguments are the beginning and the end: therefore we can give priority to only two of our arguments regardless of how many others are available.

Why invest a lot of hard work in a case, why invest any work at all, if your efforts lack focus and direction? Much of your energy will be wasted if you spread it out over all of your case evenly. When you isolate the few critical points, emphasize them, and pour most of your energies into their development, your presentation will multiply in strength. Emphasis of a few points does not mean exclusion of the rest: you should include all the evidence you have. But establishing an effective theory of the case requires that you arrange your priorities so that the more significant an item is, the more attention it receives. And, normally, there are only a few items in any case with a significance that deserves heavy emphasis.

In Martha's problem with her in-laws, she might assign priorities in this order: (1) her relationship with Paul, (2) a pleasant relationship with in-laws if complaints are a temporary problem, (3) her feelings and defense of her actions, and (4) a pleasant relationship with in-laws if complaints are permanent. Most important is her relationship with Paul. If she notices the conflict having any adverse effects on their relationship, she will take any measures necessary to head off the trouble. If they have to pick up and move several hundred miles away to reduce the amount of contact with Paul's parents, preserving their relationship takes priority over preserving their homestead.

Yet it is unlikely that the problem will become that extreme. Since adjustments to transition in the in-laws' lives are a main source of their complaints, Martha could decide to give priority to maintaining a pleasant relationship with them over defending herself and expressing her feelings. Temporarily, she will be tolerant while a more permanent pattern of criticism would cause her to voice her objections.

In taking a case, a lawyer may end up fighting for a client's rights, counseling a client about a proposed course of action, or negotiating with others for a client's position. Because a number of distinct activities characterize the functions a lawyer performs, he or she must analyze a case right after being retained in order to determine the precise services to provide. The lawyer must settle on the best strategy for helping a client reach the desired goal. Because of the necessity to focus specifically on the goal and predict the most effective way to reach it, developing a theory of the case is almost second nature to the lawyer.

With experience in dissecting cases and judging the relevance of evidence, the lawyer also has a boost toward assigning priorities. Relevance measures probativeness. The more probative the evidence, the more significant it is in establishing a case and the more emphasis the productive attorney places on it. We admire accomplished attorneys for their ability to get to the heart of a matter. The incisive analysis that lawyers display because of training and job demands boils down to the habit of assigning priorities to the items in a case.

In either an argument with an adversary or an attempt at persuasion, you will benefit from developing a theory of the case and assigning priorities according to your theory. Usually, there are a number of different strategies available that will fit your case. In fact, it is probable that the number of arguments available to you will exceed the amount of time you have to present them or will threaten the clarity you wish to maintain in your message.

Identify the arguments with the most clout. Settle on the strategies that further your theory of the case. When you mark off the crucial territory, you can afford some flexibility in the hinterlands of lesser relevance. Like Lincoln, you can concede several weaker points in exchange for the one that is crucial.

Chapter 20

Look for
Hidden Motives

A man generally has two reasons for doing a thing—one that sounds good and a real one.

—*J. Pierpont Morgan*

You recently talked with your broker, who strongly recommended that you buy Conglomerink heavily. She thinks it is about to run up out of sight and establish itself as one of the leading glamor stocks on the market. You did not count the number of times she said "ground floor," but she couldn't have touted the purchase much more enthusiastically. She predicted that Conglomerink would demonstrate why so many people continue to regard the stock market as a worthwhile investment through times of lean return. She advised you to sell your entire holding of Conglomerex and smaller amounts of various other stocks in order to load up on Conglomerink.

You reminded her of her enthusiasm for Conglomerex, which she urged you to buy last year. You wanted to test this new confidence in Conglomerink against the lessons of history. You also wanted to let her know not so subtly that her crystal ball had malfunctioned badly before. In frank tones, your broker admitted to some miscalculation.

As the ultimate consolation she mentioned that she had taken a large position in Conglomerex herself, buying almost as many shares as you did. She still believed Conglomerex would make a move, but she had underestimated considerably the length of time it had taken to shake a technical correction in the market. One man's correction is another man's fizzle, you thought, but upon her insistence that Conglomerink had all the signs of a comer, you agreed to her recommendation.

That evening, when you reviewed your checkered past as an investor, you suspected that you could have accumulated capital faster with a passbook savings account. You were chagrined to discover that you would have preserved your capital better by depositing it in your mattress. So many transactions had occurred, and yet the prize for this flurry of trading was a net loss, the booby prize. And your figures did not even include your broker's commissions.

Then the fog lifted from your brain. You went back over your figures and calculated the size of the commissions. Your broker could make it as a circus ringmaster. She had trained you as a juggler, and your act had become a command performance for her benefit alone. Each time you dropped a juggling pin she was there to pick it up, receiving a commission on each sale as you piled up your sizable minuses.

You went over the timing of the transactions in your mind. Even in retrospect, no logical pattern appeared to justify the moves. The stocks continued to pursue the same random course afterwards as before. No dramatic changes, no trends, not even a hint of significance rescued your broker's judgment.

The market was generally calm with moderate breezes blowing elsewhere. Your ship had sailed into the doldrums of the market and was going nowhere. Meanwhile, your broker steamed along at a rapid clip under the power of your commissions. Either the times had passed you by, or you needed to chart a new route. As long as you could not claim your broker as a tax exemption, you decided that you could no longer afford to invest.

You could not prove that your broker was treating you as a meal ticket, but you sure couldn't prove any market expertise either by the record of transactions. The shabby record did indicate that you had lost money while your broker had gained, and this because your suspicions lagged behind the telltale events.

We live in a complicated world in which our values and even our morality are intermingled with materialistic desires. This mixture happens to those with the best of intentions. Those with quieter superegos and fewer scruples pay greater obeisance to the dollar. And a depressingly large minority remains who put the almighty dollar on a pedestal. In simpler times, in every age, people have acted for hidden motives. We cannot stop deceiving ourselves, nor are we ready to erase deception from our dealings with others.

In our more complicated world, we should assume that hidden motives will play a fundamental role in the majority of our dealings with those beyond our circle of friends. Usually, those hidden motives will have an economic basis. The pressure on us as consumers, the emphasis to acquire, discard, and reacquire, and the dominance of materialistic values cause most of us to spend too much time chasing the bucks. We regret the choice when we must run over another to grab more dollars, but we do it just the same. Maybe we feel that buying a few more things will help us to bury the guilt.

In order to protect your interests, you must look for hidden motives in those you are dealing with. Usually, you can also trace other people's stakes back to some economic incentive. Other hidden motives such as the desire for power or influence, the need for approval and acceptance, or the pull of emotions such as revenge or pride may also underlie their actions.

Be slow to accept apparent motivation. A respectable rationale is easy to devise and will accompany every action. Suspend your belief and probe deeper for the real reason behind the action. In fact before you become involved in the action, ask yourself at the beginning, "What's in it for the other person?"

If you are in an adversary situation, analyze your opponent's stake in the outcome. Bureaucrats guarding the money of anonymous taxpayers will offer less resistance than those who must pay out of their own pockets. The same animal that will retreat quickly when an exit appears will fight ferociously when cornered. Ask yourself, "Why is this person doing this?" Then continue asking "Why else?" until you run out of maneuvering room. In some interactions you can ask the other person "Why?" and "Why else?" directly and gauge the responses.

In an attempt at persuasion you may have to overcome what salespeople call the hidden objection. The reason a prospect gives for refusing is often an excuse that sounds better or will satisfy the salesperson easier than the real reason. Saying you do not need a product will spark a sales pitch where saying you cannot afford it might avoid one. Salespeople have found that the reason given is often a justification that disguises the real reason motivating the prospect. Successful salespeople search for the hidden objection because they know they will get the sale if they can answer that objection. When you have located the hidden objection that motivates the other person, you can work with it and even supply justifications of your own for the other person to use in overcoming resistance.

Evolution has driven many of our emotions underground. They have not disappeared but we channel them into socially acceptable outlets. The jungle fighter has become obsolete, replaced by the manipulator. Gamesmanship is the contemporary form of combat. The operative word describing both the change in behavior and the measurement of the new behavior's success is "cool."

The modern actor remains unflaggingly polite; however, the disparity between surface manners and actual emotions has widened. Violent struggles ensue under a veneer of small talk and pleasantries. No one gets excited during the joust. No one becomes ruffled by wounds received or inflicted.

The popularity of tennis symbolizes this shift. Fierce head-to-head competition is played out in an atmosphere of sportsmanship. Players are polite and restrained; the complimentary recognition of their opponents' nice shots delineates the surface. The strains of warfare run deeper. Aggression, the vanquishing of the foe, and the exuberance of the victory dance are private experiences locked up in the mind as tightly as Victorian sexuality.

The reign of coolness makes the task of looking for hidden motives as large as it is important. As long as your competitors know the real reason for their actions and you do not, you struggle with a handicap. Discovering the hidden motives gives you an advantage, especially when your competitor is not aware of your discovery. You can follow the scenario constructed around the apparent motives—the justification—while you aim your tactics at the real reasons, which will decide the result of the conflict.

Think of how the pool hustler operates, for example. He offers friendly competition, suggesting a mild wager to make it more interesting. He lets you win the early contests, convincing you of your ability and inconspicuously building the evidence of his own ineptitude. When you are confident of your superiority, he raises the stakes and moves in for the kill. At this point the amount of money you lose depends on how long you foolishly believe that the hustler has just hit a run of luck.

However, you get taken only because you are ready to take him. When you spot a hustle, you ignore your greed and decline the bet, or you control your greed and retire after you are handed the early victories. Look for the hidden motives to protect yourself from getting hustled. Turn your discovery of hidden motives to your advantage by working on the hidden motives while you string along with the advertised ones.

Big city police speak of cynicism as an inevitable occupational hazard. Dealing with the unpleasant side of life day after day leaves them with a distorted view of human nature and engenders a callous acceptance of misery. Lawyers also see a select slice of life. Their occupational hazard is skepticism, a necessary tool of the trade.

Clients entrust the protection of their money and property to the attorney, who then stands guard over the client's economic well-being and fends off hostile claims. The attorney cannot afford to take people at face value. Too many of them are after something that must be kept secure. A lapse into naiveté breaches the lawyer's duty to the client. The attorney must constantly search for hidden motives and must nourish this worldly wise skepticism to protect the client. The lawyer is like a bodyguard, rippling with muscles of skepticism.

In addition, the general attitude of lawyers habitually demands evidence for a case, support for an argument. They doubt until they can be shown. They expect hidden motives until they find good faith and proper intentions. Adopt this attitude yourself when you are protecting your own property or any other kind of valuable. You should follow the lawyer's lead and reserve judgment until you can be shown that another's motives are sincere.

So far we have examined the search for hidden motives of which the other person is aware. Sometimes the motives for behavior are hidden even from the other person. There are significant parts of everyone's character that he or she is not willing or is afraid to recognize. When you can identify an unconscious hidden motive influencing another person's actions, you have gained a tremendous advantage, whether you seek to best the person in a conflict or persuade him or her to follow your message. You can call upon that motive to work for you, and your opponent will not be able to counteract or resist its effects.

Suppose you want to convince Bob, your neighbor, to split with you the cost of a fence between your properties. You know he does not care for a fence and will protest the expense. Yet you are tired of his dogs leaving foul presents on your lawn and jumping on you with dirty paws and sharp nails when you enter or leave your house.

You have diagnosed a case of status consciousness in your neighbor. Endorsements determine Bob's purchases as he tries to stay current with trends. He emulates those who he believes have the highest social positions. Nevertheless, he believes that his own tastes and preferences govern his actions and is not conscious of his status-seeking motives.

Your job is to portray the fence as a status object. You mention how attractive the homes are of certain leading citizens of the area, calling his attention to the appeal the fence adds. You tie up the ideas of privacy and exclusiveness with people who have attained much and who have earned the admiration and attention of others. You show him the new, expensive subdivision that is enclosed by walls. You point out the reclusive tendencies of national celebrities in show business, sports, the arts, or a field of his interest. You arrange to be found perusing an article praising fences in a slick architectural or design magazine, and then you drop a reference to the appearance of more fences as a part of landscape planning in trendy places. Your persistent message subtly delivered may soften him up to the point where he puts up the fence on his own.

Persuasion aimed at hidden motives has a more lasting effect because messages geared to the other person's frame of reference make a large impression and are remembered longer. Those messages not geared to the other person's frame of reference are soon forgotten. Find a connection between your message and the existing beliefs and experience of your listener. Information offered by itself without the accompanying support of listener appeal will change few attitudes. People are more willing to accept ideas that mesh with their own habits of thought. We saw this earlier in the stress placed on locating the common ground between you and your listener. Put your message in personal terms—those of the person you are addressing.

If you have discovered hidden motives in other people that they do not know about, you are on the offensive and can take advantage of this weakness. If you have discovered hidden motives in others that they do know about, you are usually on the defensive and can subvert their purposes. In either case they will offer less resistance if you can draw them into a discussion and avoid the atmosphere of confrontation found in debate. A discussion in which you involve other people tends to soften their resistance and achieve a more permanent effect than a debate, a speech, or a one-sided sales pitch.

The reason for the difference is that attempts at domination are naturally resisted, and an indirect approach is more effective. Discussion enables you to indirectly convey your message by planting your ideas and encouraging their expression in the other person. You try to make your ideas seem a product of the initiative of others. Let them draw your conclusion for you if they will. They will not be able to resist their own suggestions.

In working on another's recognized or unrecognized hidden motives, you are appealing to the dynamic force of self-interest. You can use the driving power of the other's motivation the same way that diplomats negotiate for their home countries. Nations, like people, act according to what they see as their best interests. When diplomats sit down at a conference table, they try to show the other side that their proposal furthers the other's self-interest.

A person's self-interest fits into two broad motives—a desire for gain and a fear of loss. These motives start wars among nations and propel individuals into action. Look for the desire for gain and the fear of loss hidden behind the actions of others. Use these motives to your benefit by identifying your position with the self-interest of the other person.

Oriental methods of self-defense apply this principle to physical force. Not only can you ward off an attack easily by using the opponent's own weight, but you can inflict damage in doing so. Hitch your argument to your adversary's self-interest and use the weight of this motivation to carry you to your goal. Desire for gain and fear of loss are among the strongest weapons you have in establishing your own case.

To keep in mind the importance of looking for hidden motives, remember the catchword *cool*. In the age of cool, the gap between apparent motives and emotions and the actual motives concealed beneath the cool exterior has widened. Remain cool and removed from the action until you have unearthed the hidden motives. Beware of the pervasive influence of cool cash. The low-key approach of discussion surpasses hot debate as a method of mining the hidden motives of another The coolness of indirectly appealing to other people's desire for gain and fear of loss uses the force of their self-interest to your benefit. Looking for hidden motives will earn you your own coolness—the highest contemporary honor.

Chapter 21

Compromise: The Art of the Possible

The better part of valor is discretion.
                        —William Shakespeare

The neighborhood is up in arms. Two children have been hurt crossing Busy Street within the last six months. Many drivers use Busy Street as a through street even though it cuts through a quiet, residential area. There is a long stretch uninterrupted by traffic signals, and the sparse cross traffic presents little interference. Because the police do not patrol the street, drivers can cheat on the low speed limit. Especially when traffic backs up on Main Avenue, a steady stream of cars whizzes past the children playing nearby.

Local residents have complained loud and often about the problem. They want the city to install a traffic light midway down the stretch at Cross Street. Dick Green, the city manager, has listened sympathetically to their requests and explained patiently on many occasions that there is no room in the budgeted highway funds for additional expenses. He suggests they renew their request for a traffic light when the new budget comes up for discussion next year. Unfortunately, the city manager does not live anywhere near Busy Street and has no personal stake in the decision. You cannot argue with his figures or his logic unless you live in the affected area and feel the need personally. Direct pressure on the manager will not work because he is an appointed, not elected, official and enjoys wide general support for the good work he has done.

The residents have taken their request for a traffic light to the mayor, an elected official who has neatly sidestepped the issue and kept it in the city manager's corner. They have exhausted every forum they could think of. They have written letters to the newspaper, appealed to state and federal officials, and approached community groups. Local business organizations have told them they favor the status quo because it eases traffic tie-ups in the business district.

Everywhere they have run into the same problem—they are a small minority of the city's population. Other people feel that too much money is involved for such a local concern. Despite the residents' fears, resignation has grown. They have begun setting their sights on a concentrated fight during next year's budget hearings.

Negotiation is a delicate art. It is as fine and almost as mysterious as courtship and lovemaking. The interplay of personalities, the battle of wits, and the clash of wills offers unparalleled challenge. Negotiation combines all the elements that you find in poker, chess, and athletic competition. Like many fascinating games, negotiation has a few basic rules that are simple and easy to follow. The three most important are to (1) start fast, (2) run hard, and (3) settle for what's possible.

Start fast. After you set your goal for the negotiation, build your strongest case by reaching well past your goal. Shoot for the sky, and let the only boundary for the length and breadth of your demands be your ability to present them credibly. If you do not think you can sell an improbable point sincerely, leave it out. A second-rate sell job will damage your other points and detract from your image as an accomplished advocate. Any relevant point that you can argue sincerely should be included even if you are not interested in winning it. You can offer it as a concession later on, maybe instead of a point you would hate to give up.

Constructing the strongest credible case on your subject provides you with bargaining leverage. There is no more necessary companion than leverage in negotiation. Leverage fuels the machine and greases it for smooth operation. Without leverage you might walk away from the bargaining table with nothing more than the polite attention of your adversary.

The local residents would have presented a more potent case if they had compiled a list of demands instead of limiting their request to a traffic light. Besides the traffic light, they could have sought heavier police patrols, a radar speed trap, ridges built up on the road to jolt speeding cars, cautionary signs, and a publicity campaign by the city to inform drivers of the problem.

Run hard is the second rule of negotiation. You do not compromise your performance. Compromise pertains to the give-and-take that occurs as a result of the bargaining. It is crucial to understand that the place for compromise is at the end of the bargaining. Proper timing in recognizing when bargaining ends marks the skillful negotiator. There is no room for compromise in the toughness of your fight during the bargaining.

The danger lies in compromising too soon. You will give away more than you should if you look for a compromise at the first sign of an impasse. Negotiation includes willingness to travel all the way to the brink. If you are running hard, you should be able to run right through the first several impasses until you get to the one that counts. When everyone is tired—tired of each other and ready to throw up their arms in frustration—the real work can commence.

Settle for what's possible is the third rule of negotiation. Compromise enters here. The best negotiator is the ultimate realist. Your most cherished expectations must give way to obtainable objectives. You can fight for the ideal goal, but you must not insist on it in the face of entrenched resistance backed up by unfriendly facts. A rigid persistence in your position without continuously testing its feasibility may result in your getting little or nothing for your efforts. You must remain flexible in order to obtain the maximum mileage for your demands.

Compromise is the art of the possible and not the art of the necessary, the just, or the desirable. If you have given yourself bargaining leverage, at this point you can begin pulling the levers.

You can offer concessions and look to your adversary to make concessions. You will shed no tears if these concessions are on points dear to your opponent while you retreat from the superfluous.

You want to draw as much attention as you can to the concessions you make and their significance as you make them. Pain may show in your features, and fanfare may accompany the announcement of your foolhardy generosity. On the other hand, your opponent's concessions should be received with mild presumption and nonchalance. Downplay them. Let it be known that, of course, you expected a retreat from such an obviously untenable, unreasonable position.

Do not dwell on it once these concessions have tallied on the scoreboard. Shift back to your generosity, perhaps by reviewing the wonderful ground you have given up so far. In bargaining place the emphasis on yourself when you discuss the past, but place the emphasis on your opponent when you discuss the future.

The idea behind negotiation is that both sides give ground to settle competing interests. There is muscle on each side. You can't be a perfectionist. You cannot seek a shutout. You are a pragmatist, looking for a victory.

What is the best possible result which the neighbors should be happy to settle for? With the tight budget and the lack of communitywide support, they should be satisfied with the installation of stop signs and stepped-up police patrols. The demand for a traffic light should clearly head up their list but cannot remain a rock-hard demand. They can compromise down to a stop sign and still slow the traffic. The city can compromise up to a stop sign and hold the cost to a minimum while providing greater safety and responding to the needs of some of its citizens. While the citizens do not have a lot of leverage in this bargaining, they will improve their position by going to the city manager with a list of demands led by the call for a traffic light and being prepared to settle for stop signs.

Most of our everyday actions follow the rules of compromise. We work hard and temporarily compromise our leisure or sometimes our peace of mind. We haul ourselves from the warm comfort of sleep and trudge through a cold, rainy Monday morning because we have a job to do. We compromise the quality of our work at times because occasional indulgence seems preferable to the more elusive goal of excellence. We set our goals high and run hard toward them. We dream of what might be.

Our limitations and the competition of the marketplace persuade us to settle for what can be. We covet the luxury coupé with chrome-plated dipstick or fiery roadster with roaring speed, but settle for the roomy family car with sporty styling, some extra options for the feel of luxury, and a manageable price tag. As long as we do not compromise too soon or too easily and we strike the best bargain available in the situation, compromise is the rational choice.

Unfortunately, the word compromise has picked up negative connotations. We associate it sometimes with giveaways and shattered principles, but until we reach a more perfect world, we should not thumb our noses at compromise. It is the dynamic principle of democratic government. The give-and-take of competing interests fashions the moderate programs that the greatest number of people can live with. It would be nice if there were enough room for each of us to rule as enlightened and benevolent dictators. Yet it is already plenty difficult for all people to get along even with compromise handy to avert unnecessary confrontations.

Standing before the judge, the defendant, recently convicted for the first time, awaits sentencing. The muffled sobs of his family filter through the heavy silence of the courtroom from the back benches. The judge glances over the rap sheet as she recalls her impressions from the trial and reflects on the testimony. The last tugs and clashes of warring imperatives delay the announcement of her decision.

Society must be protected from criminal actions. A person who has committed a crime should be rehabilitated to resume a productive place in society, and yet a criminal should also be punished. An innocent family, dependent for support on the head of the household, must make their way alone during this period. The taxpayer must underwrite the massive costs of jail, and an innocent victim deserves retribution. Enforcement of the law fosters respect for its dictates. A sad realization—that an over-

crowded prison with the bad influence of habitual offenders will
not rehabilitate—hangs over the entire decision.

Compromise is often tougher than clinging to the straight and
narrow of a philosophy. However, the art of the possible can soar
beyond the highest attainments of sticking to the same viewpoint
throughout. The judge can no more send the defendant up for a
maximum trip than she can release him outright to his family. The
best result in this no-win predicament will grow out of a wise
compromise.

The rules of compromise also contribute to effective persuasion.
You can increase your credibility as a persuader when you face
hostile listeners by compromising your message. You compromise
your message by arguing against it in part at the beginning in favor
of conflicting opinions that your listeners hold. You present both
sides of the issue when you expect the listeners to resist your
message. You should season your message gratuitously with irrelevant opinions held by your listeners. Humor is an excellent tactic
to narrow the gap between your message and the listeners'
opinions, inviting them to compromise their resistance for the
sake of the bond your humor creates. Appeals to fair play are another effective invitation for them to compromise. These devices
build your credibility.

Having laid such a foundation, you create your leverage when
you seek the change in the listeners' opinions by asking for more
change than you want. Studies show that the more change per-
suaders ask for, the more change they are likely to get if their
credibility is strong. Compromise seems to be an inherent characteristic of human thoughts. If you strengthen your message
beyond your objective, your listeners may well accept a message
corresponding to your objective.

Two central processes govern human interactions—competition
and cooperation. Each is likely to be present in varying degrees in
any purposeful human action. Competition provides incentive: it
encompasses the need for recognition, the tendency toward aggression, and the excitement of the contest. The incentive of competition leads to cooperation, the necessary link to reaching a goal.
The joint effort in cooperation enables the highest accomplishment.
Cooperation satisfies the need for association, the desire to be

liked, and the drive to follow an action through to its fulfillment.

The bargaining process acts upon competition and cooperation. Compromise tempers competition and forges cooperation. It does not tame the competitive urge so much as it controls it. Cooperation can exist only so long as a potential benefit for each party looms at the end of their interaction.

The sale of a house exemplifies the roles of competition and cooperation. The seller and buyer are competitors. The seller wants to receive the most money possible for the house, and the buyer wants to pay as little as possible. Yet they must cooperate. The seller needs a buyer, and the buyer needs a house. The seller offers the house at the highest price the market will tolerate. The buyer makes the lowest offer for purchase that will not insult the seller. Although they remain competitors throughout the bargaining, the period of cooperation begins as they compromise their disparate positions further with each counteroffer. Finally, their compromising leads to a mutually satisfactory sale price, and their cooperation has led each to satisfaction.

The description of the workings of competition and cooperation introduces an important point about compromise. You want to settle for what is possible, not for second best. In order to compromise your position the minimal amount and avoid a giveaway, you have to analyze the blend of competition and cooperation in your adversary. Depending on your adversary's personal style (some people are difficult or even impossible to bargain with) and the state of your interaction, either competition or cooperation will predominate.

The higher the percentage of competition present in the blend of the two qualities, the less compromise is possible. The more cooperation is present, the greater is the opportunity for compromise and for an advantageous result. Think of the other party's attitude as a continuum with competition at one end and cooperation at the other. You must gauge your adversary's location along the continuum to determine if conditions are favorable for bargaining.

An example: you are the prospective buyer of a home, and the seller's price is set at $55,000. The fair market value is $50,000. You offer $47,000. The counteroffer is $54,500. You sense trouble, and begin creeping up very slowly with your offers. Ultimately, the seller will not dip below $52,000; so you look elsewhere for a place to live. When you notice the competitive instincts in your opponent rising to the top, you have to be patient. Hold your ground until the signs of cooperation appear, and the climate becomes more favorable to compromise.

There is also a hint in this for your own bargaining prowess. To the extent that you can camouflage your competitive urges during bargaining, you should do so. Disguising your competitive objectives and parading a cooperative style will inure to your benefit. Showing a consistently cooperative attitude will soften your adversaries into concessions. Just because you do not exhibit competitive attitudes certainly does not prevent you from holding them and letting them push you on to prevail over the other party.

Bargaining leverage obtained from a list of demands and an overbuilt case at the beginning helps you to appear cooperative. You can make concessions and seem to give ground without doing so. When your opponents cannot decipher a competitive challenge, they will not be incited to respond in kind. When cooperation is all they see, their own competitiveness will diminish.

Finally, we consider compromise as a method of co-opting your opponents. At times we need a way to compromise the strength of their case or the thrust of an argument. We call this use of compromise anticipatory rebuttal. Anticipatory rebuttal covers two tactics: (1) answering an argument we are sure our opponents will make before they have a chance to offer it, in order to compromise its effect; and (2) conceding an argument we have no chance of winning before our adversaries make it so we can give a sympathetic account, increase our credibility, and earn goodwill.

The first tactic should be used sparingly because it is a reaction rather than an action and could cost us the initiative in a contest. We should spend more time on advancing our own case and putting our opponent on the defensive. However, the primary objection to answering an anticipated argument is that we could be wrong about our opponent's resolve to use the argument, and unnecessarily weaken our position. The tactic is useful when we have no doubt our foe will offer the argument and we can answer the argument concisely and clearly. If so, keep sight of priorities and emphasize your side of the case.

The second tactic of conceding an argument in advance poses the same danger but to a lesser degree. The second tactic is also known as the strategic admission. We saw its features earlier: you take the wind out of your opponent's sails by admitting to a smaller transgression or conceding an inevitable conclusion. Less damage results because you are able to supply the most sympathetic account, and your credibility is enhanced by a confession. You might well leave the impression that this is the only weakness in your case because you would confess to whatever there was.

The Greek mathematician Archimedes pronounced that with a large enough lever he could move the world. The modern business executive recognizes the value of leverage in making money and knows that a company without any debts is not managed well. Someone who does not employ the leverage of other people's money will never become rich. You, as a bargainer, must use leverage to accomplish your objectives. Compromise, the art of the possible, wields the lever.

There is a gulf between what you want and what you can get, between what ought to be and what can be. Settle for what is possible. Compromise is not a dirty word when it follows tough bargaining and pays off with the optimum result. Rigidity is the dirty word. When you are as stiff as a corpse in insisting on what you want, your efforts will wind up at a dead end.

Chapter 22

Establish Your Own Style

Men differ less in the sum of their abilities than in the degree to which they use them.

—Charles Darwin

Who is your favorite comedian? Woody Allen, Lily Tomlin, W. C. Fields, Jack Benny, Bill Cosby, Will Rogers, or one of hundreds of other great entertainers? You may well find that many or all of the people listed have had the ability to make you laugh. Look over the list with an eye toward style. Notice the vast differences among these comedians in the way they create humor. Each has or had a distinct personal style. Trademarks such as Fields's drinking or Benny's miserliness help to establish that unique style. Yet no one who has carved out an individual style need worry about securing a trademark to protect this style from imitation. Imitation is shallow and ineffective; duplication is impossible.

Style belongs to the individual because it grows out of the distinct traits that make up personality. It would be foolish for Jerry Lewis to copy Victor Borge's act, and it would be futile for a newcomer to try to copy the successful, individual style of an established comedian. You can steal a joke from someone else, but the style, the characteristic manner of expression, or the personality cannot be appropriated without an extreme distortion.

When you try to mimic the character you admire in another's style, you often end up displaying a crude caricature.

The most effective style you can exhibit comes from within yourself. It evolves from the exclusive features of your own character. Even a good imitation of someone you respect who has great style cannot match the grace and power contained in the honest expression of your own style.

Develop your own attributes. Establish your own style. Be yourself. No one else can do the job you are capable of. You will finish a miserable second to anyone you try to copy. Imitations, substitutions, and copies turn people off, but the real thing, the genuine article, and an original have a special attraction.

When you try to pigeonhole your presentation according to another's style, you run into several disadvantages. First, the presentation will seem artificial and will create a negative impression. Second, because you are acting out another's part, consistency will be hard to sustain. Your natural style will continuously fight for expression against the unfamiliar manner you have adopted. Third, your attempts to maintain the charade will distract you from your task and undermine your concentration. Your efforts to be consistent in the unnatural style require some fraction of your conscious attention.

The unique voice each person possesses does not grow like a hothouse plant, however. You originate your own style. Yet emulation helps its evolution. The trick is to apply the best methods of expression that others have developed to your own personality rather than fitting your expression into another's personality. Role models are healthy and advance individual development, but slavish role playing is unhealthy and inhibits development.

Parents provide role models for their children. A boy wants to grow up to be a daddy, so he mirrors the behavior of his father. Yet, extreme role playing can degenerate into mental illness: a man who walks around with one hand tucked into his shirt and thinks he is Napoleon, for example, has probably lost his perspective. Immoderate role playing, while not always disturbing to sanity, does rob a person of potential and stifle creativity.

We learn from others by building on their experience and accomplishments. But we must reach for the stepping-off place where we can set out on our own. A composer begins as a musician, playing the pieces of the masters. He or she appreciates their triumphs, trying as much as possible to understand what makes the music of the masters memorable and how they succeeded in putting the parts together to construct the stunning whole.

Then, upon reaching the stepping-off point, he or she applies the knowledge gained from predecessors (who earlier accepted a similar challenge) to his or her own labors. The beginning composer's emulation and study mature his or her own talent to create original music. Can you recognize the influence of others? Sure. The young composer may employ some of the techniques of others exactly in a new composition. However, it remains his or her piece; the composer has applied the techniques to unique ideas and expressed them in an individual style.

The application of the successes of others to our type of personality is desirable. The influence of more experienced and more able models bolsters our style; substituting the imitation of another's style in place of our own, however, brings trouble. Our aim is to learn how lawyers argue. By applying the techniques lawyers commonly practice, we should improve our own ability to advocate our position. We are not trying to be lawyers or what we think a lawyer is. That is too stiff a sentence. We do want to be lawyerlike in our arguments. We want to apply the strong features of the professional advocate's style to our own style.

Now let us look at some general principles that should assist you in establishing your own style. There are different methods for delivering your pitch: you can speak impromptu, extemporaneously, with written aids, or from memory. Impromptu means you hang loose and wing it. You head into the fray with an open mind relying on your wits to supply the needed arguments. By extemporaneous we mean that you carry no prepared remarks or written aids with you. You go over your subject in advance and select the important points and arguments, but you allow the chemistry of the moment to create the particular expression of your ideas. Written aids could consist of sketchy notes, an outline of your ideas, or even your entire presentation written out for you to refer to at times. Last, you can memorize your full presentation and give it verbatim.

Each of these methods could serve your purposes in certain instances. However, extemporaneous delivery of prepared ideas generally produces the strongest impression. Avoid memorizing unless you have a good reason for it, as it often comes out stiff, and you can get in trouble if you forget a part. The use of written aids can help a beginner or a nervous advocate as the notes provide security as well as a reference point. An impromptu approach may save extra work in a minor case, but remember that preparation is essential when anything valuable is at stake.

An extemporaneous style benefits from the support of preparation while it conceals the preparation and leaves an impression of authority and expertise. You seem to be talking with your listener and not at him—a crucial difference. Your effectiveness will not suffer because your efforts in preparation do not show. Studies have shown a conversational style to be as persuasive as a dynamic formal presentation.

Experts in rhetoric and behavior largely agree on the common features that make any style interesting to listeners. Risking repetition of earlier points, let's briefly go over a checklist of important ingredients in style.

1. Basic clarity. If the message is not clear to the listener, all else is wasted.
2. Variety in delivery and expression of the message.
3. Significance of the message itself.
4. Tailoring to the interests of the listeners. Make it seem important to them.
5. Concreteness and vividness. Use figures of speech and examples to bring the message alive. Similes, metaphors, analogy, and personification spark interest and add a visual dimension to your message.
6. Suspense or conflict leading to a resolution. Use the pull of "What happens next?"
7. Humor and folksiness to sell yourself. Your listeners want to accept your message when they like you.

Effective style varies according to the medium of communication. A spoken message will emphasize different qualities from a written message. When you prepare for an extemporaneous presentation, think of how you would say something instead of how you would write it. Think of how it sounds rather than how it looks on a page.

If you are speaking instead of writing, you will be more engaged personally with your audience, so you should use more first and second person pronouns—I and you. Your style should be less formal: use shorter words, simpler words, colloquialisms, and contractions. Oral style should have more drama, so you include more questions, exclamations, commands, repetition, and more action words in active tenses. Immediacy of impact concerns you more than following the rules of correct grammar.

These few general principles may offer some hints for your work, but let us not obscure the main point: Establish your own style. Darwin suggested that talent is spread pretty evenly; the great divide in people separates those who use their talents fully from those who waste them. Therefore, you need not be afraid to be your own person and generate your own characteristic manner of expression. The only large risk you take is in neglecting to develop your talents.

Apply the successes of others to your own style, but pass up the deceptive temptation to imitate their style. Choose the original and leave the copy. There are as many ways to get a laugh as there are good comedians, but it is not funny when you copy someone else's style.

Chapter 23

Appearances Are Important

What you are stands over you the while, and thunders so that I cannot hear what you say to the contrary.
—Ralph Waldo Emerson

A logical fallacy with the exalted title of *post hoc, ergo propter hoc* (translation: "after this, therefore because of this") describes the error of assigning a causal relationship between events just because they happen in sequence. Because one event follows another, you cannot assume that the first event caused the second. With the wisdom of this fallacy firmly lodged in your head, you visit your friendly neighborhood attorney in order to have your will prepared. Many people who die had wills drawn up to set their affairs in order, but people had been dying for a long time before lawyers conveniently invented the will.

You are ushered into the attorney's office about twenty minutes after the appointed hour. He beckons you to a chair and continues a phone conversation. You guess he is speaking to another lawyer because of the mysterious vocabulary he uses. Every so often, he looks at you as he reacts to statements by the other person, as if to draw you into the conversation as an ally. Six or seven multi-volume sets of thick, striped-back books and many individual volumes and loose-leaf binders fill a bookcase that covers the left wall. The right wall holds seven framed certificates and diplomas of various sizes arranged symmetrically. Legal files and accordion files are piled in stacks on his desk and two nearby tables. Several files lie open, cluttering the desk with their haphazard arrangement.

The lawyer has finished his call, and he greets you. His manner is as gracious as his tailoring. After exchanging pleasantries you get down to business. He pulls a file from the open drawer of a file cabinet behind him. He takes notes on a long yellow pad as he probes your financial affairs, investigates your intentions, and learns which relatives and friends are favored. He explains the many options for disposing of your property such as bequests, trusts, and gifts. You have utmost confidence in your attorney because he uses long, involuted sentences filled with strange-sounding technical terms. His patient translations and explanations make you feel like an insider.

Several days later you return to the lawyer's office to sign the finished product. You read over the will starting with the large, ornate script at the top. The lawyer clarifies the meaning of a few especially obscure clauses. Now the ceremony begins. As you announce to the witnesses looking on that this is your will, you initial each page and sign at the end. Then the witnesses sign in turn as everyone else watches.

Appearances are important. You have confidence in your lawyer because he looks, acts, and sounds like a lawyer. Any departure from the standard image might raise doubts that would have to be accounted for. There is no necessary connection between his appearance and his competence, yet somehow the correlation usually seems present. The look of the lawyer's office, personal appearance and bearing, and the sound of the jargon all contribute to the total picture that instills confidence. You believe that he can do the job because he looks like he can do the job.

Appearances related to the will are likewise important. In order for a will to be valid, certain formalities must be followed. The will must be in writing; signed by the testator (maker) at the end; declared by the testator to be the correct will; and attested to by two (or, in some states, three) disinterested witnesses. The witnesses must watch the testator sign the will. The testator and other witnesses must watch as each witness signs. These formalities only concern the appearance of the will, not the substance of who gets what. Yet if these appearances are not exactly correct, the will is not valid, and the intentions of the testator, although clear, will be frustrated.

The formalities serve several purposes. They impress upon the testator the seriousness of the action. They add to the reliability of the proof of the will at a time when the testator can no longer be asked about intentions. They reduce the possibility of undue influence against the testator. The importance of appearances goes beyond the formalities. The testator could execute a will by finger painting on paper towels and still comply with the formal requirements. Such a will could still be valid. Even if people did not question the mental capacity of the testator, however, they might not take the will seriously because making a will is serious business and people do not deviate from standard procedures without good reason.

The lawyer's appearance and the will's appearance are important. Appearances are also important to you in advocacy or persuasion. There is no clear division between substance and form. They overlap, and each influences the other. Just as the proper golf swing produces a long, straight drive, so the proper presentation delivers an effective message. The form is the vehicle that delivers the substance. A good appearance enables your message to work on its target. When your appearance makes a positive impression on those listening, they are more apt to pay attention to the substance of your message, and your advocacy or persuasion becomes more effective. The medium is at least a good part of the message.

Many analysts have said that the 1960 Kennedy-Nixon debate was the decisive factor in Kennedy's election. The debate itself was close, but most observers gave Nixon the edge on the issues —the substance. Kennedy became president because he walloped Nixon in the contest of appearances. Kennedy appeared cool, decisive, in control, and in charge. He answered forcefully and sat passively through Nixon's answers. He looked confident, like a leader.

Nixon's makeup gave him dark, sunken eyes and a pasty, pallid complexion. He sweat a lot, and his body movements were tentative. His eyelids fluttered, and his glance darted back and forth. As he watched Kennedy's answers, his reactions did not flatter him. The contrast in appearances put Kennedy in the White House. You can argue whether this is an appropriate way to select a president. You cannot argue, however, that the contrasting images of the candidates created by the debate greatly influenced the selection. Appearances are so important to politicians that they would do without a makeup artist only if it were necessary in order to keep pollsters on the payroll.

The famous magician Harry Houdini showed how substance and appearance blend inextricably to construct the final result. The magic remains, even though we know some sleight of hand would explain the trick, because the magic resides in the artistry of the performance. We appreciate how the trick is done fully as much as the trick itself. The long hours of planning and preparation, the split-second timing, the razor-thin margin for error, and the cleverly hidden gimmick, which constitute the heart of the trick, create an appearance that in turn makes up a large portion of the substance of the trick.

The magician teaches us that things are not always as they seem only because we know deception is used to produce the effect. We are not always on guard against the deceptions of the unofficial magicians we meet every day. On the other hand, we should take advantage of the magic power of appearances ourselves to strengthen our message.

The legal profession knows the value of appearances. Look at the operation of a court. The judge dons long, flowing, somber, black robes; sits apart from the rest of people, elevated and separated by a high, large bench that obscures the distractions of the lower body; and wields the gavel, an audible symbol of authority. The dignity of wood paneling and ornate furnishings adds to the decorum.

Attending officers direct that all rise as the judge enters and command silence. Reading is forbidden. Respectful gestures are routine. The judge's name is "Your Honor." The lawyers look so similar with obligatory attaché cases that they might as well be in uniform. It is obvious that anyone who marches out of step will pay the price. A teenage ghetto dweller wears a suit for the first time in his life, because it will increase his chances of beating the rap.

Take that same judge, with the same intelligence, compassion, and wisdom, and dress him in a clown suit, or move the court into a garage, or just start calling him Jim. Can you picture the contrast in the impression that results? The journey from sublime to ridiculous reflects a change in appearances alone.

You communicate through your appearance. You communicate through your lack of concern for your appearance, too. There is no way out. You cannot choose not to play the surface game of appearances. People judge the depths by the surface appearance because they cannot see the depths. The impression you create depends on the appearance you present.

First impressions are a powerful influence on the ultimate judgment others make about you. Good looks open doors. Is that just? No. But, is it true? Yes. Other appearances work the same way. When you say something with assurance, people will more easily accept it. When you seem to know what you are doing, people will not question you as quickly. Prestige is in the eye of the beholder.

Act like you know what you are doing and like you believe in what you are saying. How can you expect another to accept what you say when you convey doubt about your message? Why should someone pay attention to your message when you are not enthusiastic about it yourself?

Do not betray uncertainty in your speech or manner. Good preparation should include any introspection you need to do, so you can battle unquestioningly and without hesitation. The trial lawyer believes in the justice of a client's cause. The lawyer may have been convinced from the beginning of the case or sometime during the research and preparation stage. Either way, the good lawyer must develop the attitude that the client is deserving in order to advocate effectively.

Our old friend Aristotle used the word *ethos* to describe the persuasive power of an individual's personality. Modern writers agree that ethos is one of the strongest factors in persuasion. Ethos describes the listener's perception of the speaker's knowledge, character, and attitude toward the listener. It is a factor of appearance. How those listening feel about you is at least as important as how they feel about your message.

Ethos requires that your presentation be sincere. Thus, you must banish doubt beforehand. Give the impression that you are winning; carry yourself as if you expect to win, and let your confidence in your message show. Do not apologize or make excuses for a weak case or lack of preparation or personal shortcomings. If you are battling an adversary, keep your composure while the other side presents its arguments or attacks you. Strive to leave the impression with the listener that you are thorough and decisive.

Sensitivity studies have established that you can determine to a large extent how others receive you. You can create your own prestige. Check your physical appearance. Improve what you can and forget the rest. Do not worry about the things you cannot change. Very often others do not notice what we consider glaring defects. They are glaring to us because we give them so much attention. The main reason others notice a defect is that we are self-conscious about it. Check your ethos. People will treat you pretty much according to the way you act. If you act like an authority, an expert, or an important person, you will very likely be received as one.

The gatecrasher's method of operation substantiates this. He dresses for the occasion; for example, he might wear a tuxedo, a suit, or jeans, depending on what other participants favor. Most notably, he acts like he belongs. He strides forward past the security guard with an air of assurance that almost dares them to bother him for his nonexistent credentials. He mingles and greets attending celebrities as close friends, sometimes puzzling them a great deal. He goes where he should not be because his demeanor reassures others he is a member of the club. The gatecrasher penetrates barriers because of the appearance he makes. One of the most famous wound up on the podium for a presidential inauguration. Let a positive appearance work for you, and you will be surprised how far it will take you.

Similar principles apply to the delivery of a message with the air of authority. If a statement is made repeatedly in a confident manner, without argument or proof, eventually it will be accepted without evidence when it is stated with authority. Adding evidence and argument to such a positive delivery makes it even more dynamic.

The present-day concern with image has become a major preoccupation. Corporations and individuals alike are sensitive to the need for creating and projecting a positive image. The information explosion and the pervasive media have enlarged on the role of image, and billions of dollars support the attempts to render the right image. The public relations field has burgeoned under the strain of the demand. Image defines the impression formed in people's minds from the appearances another presents.

Think of the prominent place image has taken in our lives if you have any reservations about the importance of appearances. Polish your own image to heighten your prestige. Your effectiveness as an advocate and your power to persuade depend to a great degree on the public relations job you do in projecting the proper image of yourself.

Chapter 24

Don't be Intimidated

Action seems to follow feeling, but really action and feeling go together; and by regulating the action, which is under the more direct control of the will, we can indirectly regulate the feeling, which is not.

—*William James*

Steve Lamb is a shy person who has survived in the world but is not thriving. He has earned a comfortable lifestyle but is not happy. He lives with an emotional turmoil resulting from unrealized and untested ambitions, and his talents far outstrip his accomplishments. Shyness has pulled him up short. He shies away from promising situations and backs down from opportunity. A strong fear of success has been bred in him.

For example, Steve lives alone and would very much like to develop a good relationship with a member of the opposite sex. Although he has dated sporadically, he is awkward with women and feels ill at ease. His attractive qualities are lost in a frenzy of nerves. After one or two dates, the women find excuses to end their uncomfortable encounters.

Steve has greatly admired an attractive, friendly, and bright woman at work for some time. In their brief, polite exchanges her manner and vitality have charmed him. In his free time, he fan-

202 / THINK LIKE A LAWYER

tasizes a life together with her, growing closer through shared experiences. His dreams teeter on the brink of possibility in the safe haven of a dimly lit apartment. But they crack in the cold, sober light of a day at work when he retreats from showing her his interest.

After weeks of trying to spur himself on and castigating himself for his timidity, he tells himself that she is not really his type. The lie is obvious even to himself, but he wants to quiet his inner turbulence. He wants just as much to avoid facing his very unpleasant opinion that *he* is not *her* type. He fears that anyone with her attributes and self-assurance would never settle for a flawed specimen like him.

In our liberated times Steve may represent an extreme case. Still, his opinion about his unworthiness has no more basis in fact than his strained conclusion that she is not his type. Having defined their relationship without testing it, Steve has gotten to the point where his actions are following his feelings. His worst fears lead to a self-fulfilling prophecy about his inadequacy. His negative feelings dominate because of his long-standing habit of allowing his feelings to govern his actions. If he had resolved to regulate his actions according to his ambitions and concentrated on this practiced course of action, his attitude would be markedly better.

In the last chapter we discussed the importance of appearance and the power of image. Now we look at the flip side of the coin. Refusing to be intimidated is the defensive counterpart to presenting a good appearance. A strong opponent will defeat you a certain proportion of the time. Imposing situations will overwhelm your capabilities. Honest setbacks are a part of competition, and you can live with that. The unfortunate defeat is self-defeat.

Intimidation causes self-defeat. You concede the fight before it begins because you fear your opponent or the situation. Feelings of fear, feelings of inadequacy, or negative feelings will regulate the action unless you control them by regulating the action yourself through the force of your will.

Enough has been said about the power of positive thinking and the need for a strong self-image. So instead of focusing on how to enhance these qualities, you may also benefit from the opposite angle of thinking about how to prevent the assault of intimidation. First, recognize that many people employ this strategy of intimidation. They are better fighters in a war of nerves than in a contest on the issues. They consciously or unconsciously seek to create a certain impression that will increase your anxiety.

Second, recognize that intimidation, your feelings about your opponent or the situation, and your predictions based on appearances are, at their core, irrelevant to the resolution of the issues in conflict. The main relevance intimidation has is to tip you off to a possible weakness of your opponent on the issues. If opponents are satisfied with their case, they will usually stick to it. Third, counteract attempts at intimidation by regulating your actions. Your feelings will follow. Put your efforts into the job at hand and let your feelings grow out of your performance.

Advocacy is active. Lawyers put their cases forward. They can't afford to dwell on their adversaries' points or reputations. They can't allow their feelings to influence their actions. They act; they argue; they present what they have in any way that they can. If either an adversary or a judge dissuades a lawyer from setting out all the evidence, that lawyer has not done the job.

What are the ways of regulating action? One of the best is overcompensation. Identify a weakness and overcompensate for it. Since intimidation frequently plagues people who are basically shy, let us use shyness as an example. Shy people should overcompensate by forcing themselves to be outgoing. Shyness leads people to believe that they are imposing on others when they initiate an action. They fear a visit might be barging in on others. They hesitate to speak, because they doubt the value or interest of their comment. They see an ordinary request they make as a burden on others.

Shy people should consciously set out to barge in more. They still will not offend people because of their starting point. Their greatest fear, offending people, is least likely to happen because of their reticence. They can safely increase the risk of offending others significantly in order to overcome their hesitancy. As shy people consciously shape their actions, they will notice that they are becoming less shy because they are not acting like shy people.

Many leaders have taken this path. Unsatisfied with their shyness, they set out to defeat it by overcompensating and found their actions taking them to prominent positions. Although fear can hinder performance when it runs out of control, paralyzing our ability to think clearly and act smoothly, it can work as a positive creative force when harnessed; the nervous edge of butterflies improves performance, for example. Controlling fear is essential, and overcompensation is one method.

Another method for regulating action, fatalism, reduces personal responsibility by ascribing the control of events to the hands of fate. This eases the pressure on us. Religion offers a similar comfort in its reliance on the wisdom of God's will. Fatalism, in this sense, is the opposite of self-consciousness. We jump into the action mindless of potentially intimidating details because the situation is out of our hands. We are actors playing out a script written by fate.

For someone susceptible to intimidation, fatalism can be an excellent refuge. Fatalism helps to regulate the action by reminding us not to take ourselves too seriously. Somehow, events always seem more important than they are when we are in the middle of them. Looking back, we wonder how we could have gotten so lathered up. Fatalism provides the same removal from events that the passage of time does. We would not read a month-old newspaper as closely as today's. Fatalism skims over the range of our feelings, deferring only to those of the highest rank. Whatever will be, will be.

Bluffing can also help you fend off intimidation. The tactic of bluffing returns to the idea of a good offense being the best defense. You seek to intimidate adversaries to prevent or balance off their attempts to intimidate you. The purpose of the bluff is to make it seem as if you know more than you do. If your opponent folds the hand, you win just as decisively with a king high as you do with three aces. A bluff must be credible; it must have a solid basis in facts to reduce the temptation to your opponent to call you on it. The effective bluff is the one that is not challenged.

You can also bluff yourself. This is also known as psyching yourself up. You assume that the favorable result will occur and proceed accordingly. There is no room for another's intimidation because you have already resolved the outcome yourself. Salespeople do this by assuming they will get the sale. Once they accept this assumption, their sales invariably increase because objections are seen as temporary and insignificant. Resistance to the sale challenges rather than intimidates the salesperson because it flies in the face of the inevitable. The customer's failure to buy must reflect a lack of understanding or an impatience with the sales pitch.

You can benefit by regulating the action right down to overseeing your physical characteristics. Fewer people will try to intimidate you, and you will put less stock in those who do, when you carry yourself properly. Poor movement, gestures, and poise are an open invitation you send for others to treat you as an inferior. Most important is eye contact. Looking the other person in the eyes as you speak shows assurance and sincerity and engenders a feeling of equality. If you pin the other person down with your gaze, he or she will not slip off into some kind of mischief.

Speak up, keep your volume up, and enunciate clearly. Express what is on your mind, and state it positively. You do not have to strain for a deep tone but stay away from a complaining whine. Avoid equivocations and mealy phrases like "kind of" and "sort of" and the apologetic tone of explanations that begin "I was just . . ." or "I was only . . ." Tentative speech, or letting your sentences trail away into a mumble, tells other persons that they need not pay attention to your message.

Some people's posture can indicate a continuous attempt to hide from others. Slouching and slumping, hunched over when they walk, these people seem to be constantly looking for a hole to crawl into. Stand up straight and walk tall, and you'll feel more confident. Others will also give you more respect.

If you shrink from others physically, the effect will carry over to your message. Face others squarely, and welcome physical contact. A good handshake, a hand on the shoulder or arm, and a pat on the back can help create a feeling of intimacy. When your movement and gestures show that you are important, people will tend to treat you that way and you will tend to feel that way. Action and feeling go together. The more forcefully and vividly you and your message are presented, the greater your influence will be.

Dare yourself to do the job. Then take your dare. A well-prepared case argued in a confident manner has a great chance at success. The amount of time spent by your adversary in being slovenly or careless and not knowing what the situation requires will guarantee you a reward as long as you refuse to be intimidated by appearances and persevere in putting forth your case forcefully.

You cannot expect others to accept your arguments if you do not show by your actions that you are convinced yourself. You cannot expect others to like you when you show that you are not sure of yourself. Intimidation is the acceptance of another's standards about your case or yourself. Intimidation will defeat you before you begin the fight, so form your own standards and act like the success you are when you meet those standards. Your feelings will follow the lead, and the rest will take care of itself.

Chapter 25

Control and Use Emotions

The times are bad. Very well, you are there to make them better.
—Thomas Carlyle

Just as a color-blind painter would operate under a serious handicap, an advocate blinded by emotions faces a crippling obstacle. Anger and passion blind and color judgment; emotions undermine perspective and interfere with effective argument.

Actors project the emotions of the characters they portray without being caught up in them, manipulating feelings to create the effect required by the drama. They do not ride the crest of their emotions to wherever they lead. The good actor controls his or her emotions and directs their course with a conscious skill. The effective advocate uses emotions in the same way.

The professional beggar plays on the emotions of prospective donors and tries to gain their sympathy. A responsive emotion converts into cash. An effective advocate also uses the emotions of an adversary or a judge to further a case.

The previous three paragraphs introduce the three ways in which emotions can affect advocacy. Advocates must control their own emotions. They should use emotions as a device to strengthen their message. They should use the emotions of an adversary to weaken the adversary's case or the emotions of a judge to make the judge more receptive to their own message. Let's take them one at a time.

First, control your emotions. Undoubtedly, this is easier said than done. This is the type of goal for which you ceaselessly strive but which you never reach. The potential is greater here than in enlisting another's emotions because your jurisdiction is stronger. The emotions are your own, and theoretically they are susceptible to your control.

You can present a better case when you maintain an emotional distance from your arguments. The sight of a gambler betting more than he can afford to lose is not pretty. He is a ball of nerves, sweating through the ordeal. Agitation overrules prudence. Advocates who do not control anger, fear, or other intervening emotions run the same risk of choking off their prudence. Do not love or hate; just do your job.

Common figures of speech describe what happens in anger: he lost his head; she flew off the handle. Common sense recognizes that emotions cut off our analytical powers and judgment. You must remain detached from your subject and cool. No integral personal involvement or identification with your arguments should affect the resources you bring to your fight. Good lawyers are sometimes likened to hired guns. This may be a backhanded compliment, but it demonstrates the dispassionate attitude effective advocates possess. It is a crime of passion for an advocate to lose control of emotions.

The second function of emotions in advocacy is to strengthen the advocate's message through their use as a dramatic device. We won't dwell on this point because for most of us it is a minor one. If you have the actor's ability to express an unfelt emotion, you are aware of it and probably take advantage of it already.

For those of us who do not come by this talent naturally, it is better to use this method sparingly if at all. A conscious attempt to reproduce a certain emotion can too easily degenerate into self-consciousness and sham. Those of us who lack the talent of feigning emotion can take comfort in the realization that the message is the important thing and acting ability counts for little in comparison.

The nature of advocacy relegates the actor's talent to the background because most cases afford the advocate an abundant source of material for genuine emotion. The natural expression of emotions appropriate to the case, growing out of your efforts to press the case, will enhance your persuasiveness. For example, if you have been taken advantage of and you are arguing as a wronged party, arguing in a flat, emotionless tone will hurt your chances: if you show no emotion, your listeners will not believe you were hurt.

Control is the key. You must express the appropriate emotions, but you must remain master of them. A distinction that preserves the advocate's detachment may help you accomplish this. The law distinguishes between ownership and use. A deed shows ownership; a lease shows the right to use.

Instead of thinking of the emotions of the case as your own personal property, regard them as belonging to the situation of the case. You have the right to use the emotions to advance your case. You set up the case itself as a separate entity, apart from yourself. This permits you to maintain some distance and head off the dangers of intimate personal involvement. You become a conduit for the expression of the emotions belonging to the situation.

Studies in persuasion show that your message will be more persuasive the more forcefully and vividly it is presented. How can you present your message forcefully without the aid of the emotional punch inherent in the facts of the case? There ought to be an emotional dimension you can draw on. If you can find no emotional content in your facts, what are you fighting about?

The third function of emotions in advocacy concerns your use of the emotions of an opponent, listener, or judge.

For the same reasons that we avoid emotional identification with our case, we welcome it in our opponents. We want to encourage emotional behavior on their part. If we are able to manipulate their feelings, we gain a significant advantage. When their feelings direct the course of their arguments, there is less room for analysis and planning.

An angry opponent is less likely to develop a strategy. Praising the strong points of an opponent's case, approach, or skill in handling the case before the fight begins may obscure your opponent's appreciation of the size of the task. A false sense of security and vanity may replace the concerted effort he or she needs in order to compete effectively.

Coaches have done this so consistently in sports that it has become a cliché. Before the big game, the coach paints such a dismal picture of the team's chances against the invincible foe that the team wonders if they should consider a forfeit. The coach raves about nothing but the strength, ability, and execution of the other team before the game. Then his team wins. A fluke? The coach's comments after the game deny it. His tone shifts 180 degrees and now he cannot say enough about how well his team played to fulfill his expectations of victory.

Using the emotions of a listener or a judge in an attempt at persuasion will occur more often than the opportunity to incite an adversary. We reiterate the belief that the feelings predominate over the intellect. You must be at least as concerned with moving your listeners with emotions as you are with convincing them with logic. If your listeners sympathize with you, they will look for a way to agree with you. If they feel sorry for you, they will try to ease your predicament. If they respect you, they will defer to your assertions. If they fear you, they will avoid crossing you. Most important, if they like you, they will want things to go well for you.

Just as in using your own emotions, the facts of the case provide the most fertile source for material to arouse a listener's emotions. Analyze your case for an emotional theme. Let's assume you find a beautiful bentwood rocker at a garage sale. It is in excellent condition. The price tag says fifty dollars and it is worth all of that. You enjoy bargaining and want to do better. You plan to offer thirty-five dollars. Which of the following five approaches do you like?

1. "Fifty dollars is too much for that old rocker. Look at this dent here and these scratches. I'll give you thirty-five."
2. "We really need a rocking chair for my husband's bad back. He's in such pain. He hurt his back at work and got laid off. So I'm afraid we don't have much money, but we could spare

thirty-five dollars. The doctor says it will give him some comfort."

3. "We have to replace all of our furniture. We lost everything in a fire. The insurance only covered half our loss, so finances are a problem, but we could pay you thirty-five dollars."

4. "That rocking chair is just like the one my mother used to have. Since she broke her hip, she has given up her home and come to live with us. She is lonely, and the rocker would give her a great deal of consolation. Her medical bills have strapped us, but we could pay you thirty-five dollars."

5. "I really want that rocker, but I promised myself I would only spend thirty-five dollars. Would you sell it to me for thirty-five?

The first and the last do not measure up to the other three approaches. The three in the middle enlist the feelings of the seller. The seller is not standing in his garage anxiously waiting to give you an eye-popping bargain. However, if he has a sympathetic reason for shrinking his take, he may be persuaded to do it and take the balance of his return in good feelings. The fancy name for this approach is an argument *ad misericordiam,* which is Latin for an appeal to sympathy.

Advertisers favor sex, babies, and pets to arouse your feelings. When advertisers use a slinky model to pat and stroke a new car, they are using your sex drive to sell the car. Also, they hope you may subconsciously believe that driving this car will make you as attractive and well noticed as the model. The advertisers want to appeal to lust and vanity. The model is not an engineer, there to point out the features of the car; she is there to show off her features and get buyers' engines going.

Say you want to convince your listener to fight against a proposed tax increase. There is nothing especially sexy about taxes, so that is not the correct approach. The appropriate emotional theme might be anger. In this case anger works differently from the way it works when you seek to incite an opponent. Usually, you provoke your opponent's anger against you; here, you arouse anger in your listener against an external object. It might be termed shared anger here to distinguish the two. If you and your listener share an anger against a third person or an outside force, this mutual anger might persuade your listener to follow your suggestions.

Politicians employ common emotional themes to win the feelings of the electorate. They translate pride and greed into votes at the ballot box. Pride enters when the politician flatters an audience: "The American people are wise, good, won't stand for it, etc." Politicians compliment, kiss babies, and are always glad to see you. Their patriotic references also appeal to pride.

Greed emerges from the pork barrel. Promises, promises, promises. The politician promises more than the puffing of an optimistic merchant—more jobs, more services, more benefits, less tax money, less government interference. You are reassured that you will get yours if you only give your vote. If you have clout, these promises might be kept. (But politicians can't keep all of their promises all of the time.)

Besides analyzing the situation for persuasive emotional content, you should also study your listener. Each person's emotional makeup is different, so each person will be susceptible to different appeals. There are optimists and pessimists. One person may respond to envy where another responds to pride. One person may react to positive feelings and love while the negative side appeals to another. Remember the persuasive power of such emotionally toned words as firm versus stubborn, outgoing versus pushy, and relaxed versus lazy.

We have now seen the three functions of emotion in advocacy: advocates must keep their own emotions in check; they should use the emotions latent in the facts of the case to strengthen their presentation; and they should use the emotions of an opponent or a listener to improve their position.

Now we will look at two secondary principles before we close up shop. The first principle is that the weaker your position, the more exaggerated your response. When the facts of the case favor your adversary, you should rely more heavily on emotional appeals and argue your case with more flourish.

An exaggerated response converts the simple and direct into the confused and intricate. A simple, direct approach to a weak case risks exposing the weakness and losing. Exaggeration conceals the weakness under extra details and the affect of style. Exaggeration includes vague words, passive tenses, many words, abstractions, hedging, and generalizing. This style deflects the specific inquiry as well as it aids the inflation of your meager strengths.

You turn the case inside out, using specific instances when you should be generalizing and generalizations when you should be specific. If you are successful, the confusion you create may prevent your adversary from establishing winning arguments. When the dust settles, the fight may already be over.

The second rule operates when the outcome is uncertain, rather than in a losing case. It is that the less you know, the more you listen. Too many cases are lost by an advocate instead of being won by an opponent because the advocate blunders into an error before finding out the lay of the land.

The accomplished competitor feels out an opponent before taking significant action. He or she gives nothing away that the opponent does not earn. Before you decide to arouse an adversary's anger, make sure he or she is not one of the people who can think coolly when angered. You may only reinforce the resolve to beat you. Listening first usually gives you the information you need to proceed safely.

The emotions supply an endless source of material for the advocate. No matter how bad the times are, you can make them better with the help of emotional appeals. When you inject the proper feelings into your case, you will feel a lot better about it.

Chapter 26

Thinking: The Hardest Labor

There is no expedient to which a man will not resort to avoid the real labor of thinking.

—*Joshua Reynolds*

In an earlier chapter thinking was viewed from the standpoint of solving a problem or searching for an idea. We discussed different approaches—brainstorming, classification, cause and effect—that can help generate ideas or solutions. Because thinking is so basic and so crucial to most of our activities, we have a sequel: we will now study thinking in a more general way by focusing on the thinking process itself rather than on specific ways to structure our thinking to track down an idea.

When we engage in hard physical labor, the effects are noticeable. We breathe heavily; we sweat, and our muscles not only feel the strain, but our expressions also show it. An observer can estimate how hard the work is by watching the symptoms of the worker.

Mental labors are more elusive. People exerting great effort in thinking can look like they are asleep, sitting stock-still with their eyes closed. There is no sign of any energy being expended. Despite outward appearances, thinking is laborious. While it is dif-

215

ficult to compare mental and physical labor, most people share the conviction that mental labor is more demanding.

The demands of thinking lead to our first important point. Physical fitness is a necessary ingredient in productive thinking. We need a good supply of energy to keep that bulb burning brightly in our brain. Proper rest, diet, and exercise preserve the body's vigor, which encourages an active mind.

World class chess competitors train like athletes to prepare for the rigors of matches. An advocate, like a chess player, is a competitor. Competition rapidly soaks up energy with its mental and psychological demands. The stamina necessary to meet those demands and see the job through without wilting comes from taking care of ourselves. Physical fitness only makes good sense.

Two qualities—concentration and persistence—stand out from the rest in drawing a profile of the process of thinking.

Choose a subject you are familiar with and enjoy. Try to concentrate on that subject alone for five minutes. Set a timer so clock-watching will not disturb you. If you last for five minutes without continual interruptions, you can skip the rest of this chapter. Most of us will suffer a bombardment of the small concerns of the day, daydreams, and urgings to escape the task. Our minds turn every which way to ideas that seemingly cannot wait. As a spirited horse rebels at the bridle, our minds fight to run free. Once a mind is harnessed, though, the amount of work it can accomplish makes the struggle to tame it worthwhile.

The ability to concentrate is neither innate nor predetermined, like height. You can develop your powers of concentration just as you can strengthen muscles. You build up a muscle through use, especially when you put a little extra strain on it. The same principle applies to your powers of concentration, which will improve through your efforts to concentrate.

As with other skills, concentration requires practice to develop. The effort need not be unpleasant. Sometimes we concentrate easily; for example, we are concentrating when we are engrossed in a good book, a movie, or a sporting event. A Sunday drive, a trip to a museum, or a hobby also require concentration. We have no problem with these because we have convinced ourselves that they are fun. The real effort in concentration lies in our attitude toward the subject, not in our mental prowess.

How can you recognize successful concentration? You can tell it because you will not be aware of your thinking or yourself until sometime after you have stopped. Solid concentration blocks out your consciousness of yourself, and you become literally lost in thought. Your absorption in the subject is like a trance except for the energy you are expending on the subject.

The other vital quality in thinking is persistence. Experts estimate that the amount of our brain capacity that we actually use is only around 10 percent. We should not be afraid of either reaching the limits of our ability or wasting our talents on nonessential information. We can safely try to push our mind to its limit because we will never get within shouting distance of capacity.

In order for your thinking to pay off, you have to be stubborn about it. Solutions come to those who have thrown themselves into a problem without reserve and who will tolerate no slackening until the job is finished. Solutions come to those who have provided no means of escape, rather than to one who decides offhand that it would be nice to solve the problem. You need a real stake in the attempt. A detached curiosity will not sustain the necessary drive.

Persistence brings your thoughts back on line with your goal when they wander. Thinking is not the same thing as mental activity. Your mind is active all the time, even when you sleep. An active mind does not imply thinking, which must be directed at a specific goal. Persistence is the ability to chase that goal through distractions until you catch it.

Certain small practices can lighten your labor in thinking. You can cut down on distractions by finding a quiet place and getting comfortable. Take care of any nagging little business of the day first so your mind will be as clear as possible when you begin. Close your eyes to avoid visual distractions.

When you write down your ideas, you will find that they register better and work harder. Make sure you know the meaning of all the terms you use. If you are not comfortable with a word or phrase, substitute a simpler synonym for it. Talk to yourself. When you carry on a dialogue with your ideas, you can more easily stick to the subject.

Break the problem down into parts and work on one piece at a time. Follow up any leads that pop into your head. Do not dismiss an idea immediately because it does not seem to fit. Usually, there is a reason for its entering into your consciousness. Make your own attempt to think a problem through before consulting others or source material. You will get a better appreciation of the problem and can assess better how others handle it.

Finally, set the problem aside when you meet an impasse. Cool off your brain so your subconscious can go to work on the information you were reviewing as well as relevant information from your experience. Even without the benefit of the subconscious, a break once in a while returns you to the work refreshed and with an improved perspective. Persistence means that you do not quit, but you can pause.

Thinking is closely linked to memory. Earlier, we discussed the role of memory and the power of association in the thinking process. We can call upon our memory to retain important information. Three factors influence our ability to store information useful for our thinking—impression, repetition, and association. We do not have a lot of control over the type of impression a fact has on us. Either it makes an impression, or it does not.

We can remember a fact by repeating it several times and associating it with other facts deeply embedded in our minds or with striking facts that have made a deep impression on us. Memory depends on use. If we do not recall a fact every so often, or at least recall another fact we associate it with, the fact will slowly fade out of our control.

The importance of understanding the thinking process for an advocate is obvious. Our treatment should also reinforce the value of distraction to an advocate as a defensive measure. Interruption or diversion of an opponent's train of thought pushes his or her goal farther away.

The easiest and most popular method of distraction is to divert the discussion to personal characteristics. A common example happens when someone starts a string of compliments flowing to another who has been discussing a topic disagreeable to the first person. Name-calling operates on the same principle as flattery, although it is somewhat messier.

The labor of thinking compares to long distance running. It is demanding, and we must repeatedly fight the temptation to quit. Yet once we hit our stride, we seem to enter an altered state of consciousness. We submerge into the task and can even experience moments of euphoria. Then, for something so difficult to master, it feels so natural. Best of all, each endeavor makes the next one easier. Every time we run, we can run a little farther or a little faster.

Chapter 27

Slough It Off

I have not yet begun to fight.

—*John Paul Jones*

Sharon Green had been squirreling away some of her paycheck every month. She knew she would never get rich on her salary, so she resolved to save enough for an investment program. She wanted an investment that offered the chance to make a major killing. She knew the prospect for a windfall carried with it a corresponding heavy risk, and she accepted that. Sharon was young, perhaps foolish, and had time on her side.

She had studied the various options for her money. Reluctantly, she ruled out investing in a business or in real estate, because she could not spare enough time from her job to supervise a business or manage a building. She decided against the commodities market, because she judged it to be an insider's game. Stocks appeared to be the best bet, as the potential return could be increased by writing options. The risk was greater but still within acceptable limits.

After two years of sacrifice and self-denial, Sharon set out to build her fortune. Lacking experience in investing, she spoke to a broker at length and listened to suggestions. She read what she could and scrutinized the analyses and advice of investment services. Finally, she chose a stock from a field with a long, time-honored tradition in speculation—mining stock.

She specifically picked a newly formed company engaged in oil exploration, using all her money to take options to buy this company's stock. Sharon was betting her entire bankroll on their striking oil, and to make a long story shorter, they did not. A number of dry wells later the company was dissolved, and Sharon's bankroll was dissolved in the process. What could she do? Next month, she made her first deposit toward her next venture.

While Sharon may still be somewhat inexperienced, she is not dumb. Her idea was sound; however, the odds ran against her. Luck did not smile on her on that spin of the wheel. But as long as the risk was worth taking, the speculator does not recriminate, but plans and prepares for the next ripe opportunity to risk again.

Competition leaves little room for sentiment. In a sense, competition is cruel, as it creates more losers than winners. When you compete as an advocate, you will sometimes lose. You can prepare exhaustively, argue eloquently, fight to the limit of your ability, and still lose.

Because of this unhappy truth, there is one more quality you need in order to function as a well-rounded advocate—equanimity, or the composure and evenness of mind to accept a loss as part of the game. It abides the unpleasant aspects of reality rather than futilely railing against events or escaping into some deadly soothing fantasy. When things sour, equanimity reminds us of the next harvest.

An attorney may try as many as ten simple cases a week. Usually, a case gets to the trial stage because the issue is a close one. The attorney should not enter any trial expecting to lose; yet with so many tight contests, a dispassionate overview would conclude that all attorneys are going to lose some of their cases.

It is essential that lawyers bounce back from setbacks and attack the next case with the same frame of mind that they have after a victory. Lawyers cannot afford to let past defeats affect them. Defeat is part of the job. If they never or seldom lose, they are not trying enough cases. They are settling cases too quickly, to the detriment of their clients' interests.

Slough it off. To win or lose gracefully is to take the first step in your preparation for the next battle. The contest is always just up in front of you. If you have lost, take any lessons the setback will furnish, and then put it behind you. If you have won, celebrate your accomplishment and move on.

Past glory has a hollow ring. Dwelling on past glory fattens you up for the kill. You live in the present and the near future. When your mind lags behind in the past, it has disengaged from the scene of the action, and you will pay the price for it. Dwelling on past defeat engenders a negative attitude and makes it more likely that you will stumble again.

Possibly most important, you cannot enjoy yourself when you are inordinately concerned with past reversals. Second-guessing your judgment, mourning your misfortune, and trying to wage lost battles over again prevent the tranquility of spirit that enables you to enjoy life. Why persist in a habit of mind that causes discomfort? If you are not having fun in what you are doing, you should re-assess your priorities. It is probably not worth the gain when you are unhappy, and it is certainly not worth the loss.

Victory and defeat do not precisely measure your performance. You are stuck with the facts of your argument. The test lies in what you are able to do with the case you are given. In competition the effort surpasses the result as the criterion of achievement. In the final analysis each person competes with himself or herself and not with the adversary. Your own standards determine your success. They are at once the most accurate, the most understanding, and the most demanding.

Salespeople speak of the rational requirements for a sale. Certain basic conditions must be aligned properly for a sale to be possible. Need or desire, price, availability, quality, and the right terms must fall reasonably into place. Without this foundation, the persuasiveness and presentation of the salesperson matter little. You must argue within a set of rational requirements in every advocacy situation. When you get a soup bone instead of a steak, see how many bowls of soup you can produce.

Forget the dusty ledger of past records, and relish the personal challenge of the contest. When you have fun, your enthusiasm for the job will naturally grow from within. Your enthusiasm will make you a better advocate.

Enjoy your advocacy or do something else. Learn what you can from your successes and failures. Slough it off and move on to the contest that is just in front of you. The youthful, contemporary American thinker Leroy "Satchel" Paige said it best: "Don't look back. Something may be gaining on you."

Index

Actions, negative feelings in, 202;
  ways of, 203–4; physical aspects
  of, 205; regulating, 202–6
Admissions, 82, 136; gaining, 83–84;
  strategic, 185
Adversary, estimating, 72, 77,
  129–30
Affinity, as affecting reliability, 110
Affirmative case in debate, 150–51
Affirmative defense, 9, 10
Age, as affecting reliability, 110
Agenda, hidden. See Premise,
  unarticulated
Alternative argument, 30–38; and
  consistency, 37; defensive use
  of, 36; defined, 32; emotional
  posture of, 33; fallback
  position in, 32, 35–36; goal of,
  35; in the law, 36–37; and
  logic, 37; reasons for, 38;
  using "even if" in, 32;
  variations, 32
Analogies, 75, 139, 190
Answers, 9
Appearances, 193–99
Archimedes, 185
Argument ad misericordiam, 211

Argument, dimensions of, 55;
  emphasis in, 47, 166–68; rules
  of, 45–49; strategy in, 45–46;
  structure in, 46–47, 140, 159–62.
  See also Persuasion
Aristotle, 95, 139, 197–98
Association, 18, 218
Attention span, 59–62, 153
Audience involvement. See
  Identification
Authority. See Jurisdiction,
  subject matter

Bargaining. See Negotiation
Big lie, 34, 161
Bluffing, 204
Brainstorming, 116–17
Brief, legal, 155–56

Capacity, as affecting reliability, 110
Carlyle, Thomas, 207
Cause-and-effect, 118–19, 139, 193
Circumvention, methods of, 74–76
Clarity, 60–65, 167; objectives in,
  60; rules of, 62–63; structure
  for, 63; and style, 64–65, 190
Classification, 117–18

226 / INDEX

Clay, Henry, 36
Colorable argument, 35, 137–38
Common ground, 72, 100, 175
Common law, 22, 51–54
Common sense, 2, 159, 208
Competition, 36, 182–84, 222–23
Complaint, 9, 10
Compromise, 36, 179–85
Concentration, 62, 216–17
Conflict, 3, 7, 15, 26, 83, 129–30,
    147–51, 157–58, 164, 171,
    203–4, 212–13; anticipating
    opponent in, 96–97, 184;
    defensive posture in, 3, 12, 16,
    27, 36, 77, 121, 150, 153, 156,
    175, 202; offensive posture in,
    3, 13, 47, 175; rule for, 80.
    See also Argument, rules of
Conrad, Joseph, 17
Consistency, as affecting
    reliability, 111
Constitution, U.S., 26, 77
Contract theory, 6
Coolness, 172, 176, 208
Cooperation, 138, 182–84
Copernicus, 25
Corbin, Arthur Linton, 155
Corroboration, as affecting
    reliability, 111
Crane, Stephen, 131
Credentials, as affecting
    reliability, 111
Credibility, impeachment of, 161
Credibility gap, 15, 106, 182, 185
Curiosity, 61

Darwin, Charles, 187
Debate, 2, 97–98, 150–51, 175
Deception, 196
Declarations, dying, 160
Deduction, 121, 139
Definition, request for, 157–58
Delay, 152–53, 158
Delivery, 198

Dewey, John, 117
Dialogues, Plato's, 14, 15
Discovery, 68–73, 152; in the law,
    68–69, 99; lesson of, 70;
    skills in, 71–74
Discretion, abuse of, 153–54
Disraeli, 140
Distinctions, 22–24
Distraction, 17, 47, 57, 74–75,
    152, 213, 218
Diversion. See Distraction
Doubt, 197–98

Einstein, 25
Emerson, Ralph Waldo, 193
Emotions, 33, 54–57, 89, 128, 172,
    202–3, 207–13; three ways
    to affect advocacy with, 208–10
Empathy, 100
Emphasis, 33, 47, 64, 166–67
Equanimity, 222
Equity, 52–55; maxims of, 52–53
Ethos, 197
Evasion. See Distraction
Everett, Edward, 59
Evidence, 46, 138–42, 148–49,
    157–61, 166–67, 173;
    circumstantial, 160; direct,
    160; five categories of, 139–41
Exaggeration, 76, 212–13
Examples, 75, 139, 190
Extension, 27, 159
Eye contact, 205

Facts, 24–25, 89–91, 123, 155–56,
    210; versus conclusions,
    108–9; defined, 107, 139;
    gathering, 105–12; identifying,
    107–9; in the law, 106,
    155–56; testing reliability of,
    109–12
Fallacy. See Logic
Fatalism, 204
Flattery, 3, 61, 219

Formalities, purposes of, 194–95
Foundation, laying the, 156–61
France, Anatole, 113

George, Lloyd, 87
Guinness Book of World Records,
    13

Hearsay, 160
Hobbes, Thomas, 67
Holmes, Oliver Wendell, Jr., 147
Houdini, Harry, 196
Humor, 75–76, 182, 190

Identification, 48, 55, 61, 92, 128.
    See also Empathy
Ignorance, confession of, 71, 158
Illustration, 139
Impeachment. *See* Credibility
Impressions, first, 197
Indirection, 15, 175
Induction, 121, 139, 140
Interest, as affecting reliability, 110
Intimidation, 202–3
Irony, 76
Issue, 6–10, 23, 98, 155–56;
    definition of, 7; framing the,
    10–12, 14–18; merging the, 8;
    modeling the, 8; shaping the,
    8; statement of, 7; tailoring
    the, 8–9, 190

James, William, 201
Johnson, Samuel, 103, 123
Jones, John Paul 221
Jurisdiction, 11–14; concurrent, 12;
    discretionary 11; personal, 11,
    14; subject matter, 11–13,
    139–41

Knowledge, first-hand, 160

Language, imprecision of, 16, 60
Lawyers, The, 112

Leverage, 179–80, 184–85
Lincoln, Abraham, 59, 79, 163
Listening, 73, 212–13
Logic, 2, 27, 37, 121, 128, 139,
    157–61, 193, 210; fallacy in,
    158–59

Maslow, Abraham, 127
Materiality, 156, 159
Mayer, Martin, 112
Mill, John Stuart, 118
Miranda rule, 24, 25n
Mootness, 12
More, Thomas, 5
Morgan, J. Pierpont, 169
Motive, as affecting reliability, 110;
    hidden, 171–76
Murphy's Law, 145

Naration, manner of, as affecting
    reliability, 111
Necessity, 10
Needs, five levels of, 127
Negative case in debate, 150–51
Negotiation, 8–9, 35, 136, 178–80,
    183–85, 210; three rules in,
    178–79

Objection, hidden, 172
Observation, power of, 124–25.
    See also Identification
Opinions, 139
Osborn, Alex, 116
Other side, presenting the, 18, 182
Overcompensation, 203

Paige, Leroy "Satchel," 224
Parent-knows-best approach, 13
Pareto's Law, 166
Past, dwelling on, 223
Persistence, 217
Persuasion, 2, 3, 13, 15, 45, 55, 63,
    120–21, 141–42, 167, 172,
    175, 182, 195, 197–99; devices

Persuasion (*continued*)
in, 55–57; empathy in, 100,
127–28; outline for, 128; and
power of delay, 153; preparing
for, 91–92; rules of, 47–49;
use of emotions in, 209–12.
See also Argument
Persuasion, burden of, 148–51
Pleadings, 9, 10
Point, getting to the, 62
Policy, 43–44
Posing the problem inescapably,
16, 83
Position, fallback, order of, 33.
See also Alternative argument
Posture, 205
Pound, Ezra, 51
Powell, Thomas Reed, 21
Pragmatist, 2, 180
Precedent, 22–26, 53, 155–56;
common law, 22, 51–54;
defined, 22; distinctions, 22–24;
practical rule of, 24–25;
predictability and flexibility
in, 23
Premise, unarticulated, 159, 161
Preparation, 41–42, 87–93, 144, 190,
197–98, 223; for conflict, 89–90;
in the law, 88–89; one-sided,
95–96; for persuasion, 91–92;
in problem solving, 115
Prestige, 197–99
Presumptions, 149–50, 160–61
Prima facie case, 148–49
Priorities, 166–67
Privacy, 77–78
Problem solving, 113–20; four
steps in, 115–16; in the law,
119–20; role of memory in,
114–15; three approaches to,
116–20. *See also* Thinking
Procedural matters, 9, 24, 25, 40–42,
137, 151
Proof, burden of, 16, 147–54
Proof by classifying, 26

Proof by eliminating, 26–27
Proof by selected instances, 27
Proof, standard of, 148–50; factors
in, 149
Property law, 7
Psyching up, 204
Psychology, 125–27

Question, begging the, 17, 161
Questions, asking, 17, 71–73, 83
Questions, leading, 84

Rationale, 141, 156
Rationalization, 56, 128
Reasonableness, 43, 106
Reasoning, legal, 2, 54, 155–56
Rebuttal, anticipatory, 184
Records, confirming of, 134–36;
keeping of, 133–37; making of,
137–38; value of, 135–36;
when to keep, 133–34
Relevance, 7, 45, 62, 74, 156–58,
161, 167, 178
Reliability of information. *See*
Foundation, laying the
Repetition, 63–64, 153, 218; altered
style of, 34, 190; defined, 33
Reply, 9, 10
Reynolds, Joshua, 215
Ripeness, 12

Salesmanship, 2, 26, 65, 172,
205, 223
Savvy, 123–25
Scientific method, 99
Self-defense, 9, 10
Self-interest, 15, 175–76
Shakespeare, William, 143, 177
Shyness, 203
Simplicity, 63
Simplify, desire to, 16
Skepticism, 126, 156, 173
Slanting, 17
Slogans, 63
Socrates, 14, 15

Socratic method, 14, 15
Specialization, and lawyers, 40–41
Stacking the deck, 27
Standing, 11
Statistics, 27, 140–41
Statute of Frauds, 142
Stories, 74
Strategy, trial, 2, 10, 151–53, 222
Style, 34, 37, 48–49, 64–65,
  187–91; disadvantages of
  imitation in, 187–88;
  evolution of, 188–89;
  ingredients in, 190; oral,
  189–91
Subject, changing the, 74
Substance, 42, 195–96; ways of
  viewing, in the law, 98–99
Supreme Court, U.S., 107n
Surprise, 61

Theory of the case, 164–168; in
  the law, 167

Thinking, 155–56, 215–19; aids to,
  217–18; defined, 114; and
  memory, 218; in persuasion,
  120–21; and physical fitness,
  216; two qualities in, 216–17.
  See also Problem solving
Torts, 43–44
Toward a Psychology of Being, 127
Transference, 27
Turning the tables, 74
Twain, Mark, 140
Two-valued orientation, 16

Utopia, 5

Whitman, Walt, 29
Word manipulation, 17–18, 159,
  212–13

Yes-or-no game, 15, 16, 72, 152
Your Creative Power, 116